ANGELS AND APPARITIONS
TRUE GHOST STORIES FROM THE SOUTH

Barbara Duffey

*To Jim,
Best wishes &
God Bless You,
Barbara Duffey*

Elysian Publishing Company

Eatonton, Georgia

Published by

Elysian Publishing Company
113 Cherry Point
Eatonton, Georgia 31024
706-485-0741

All photographs were taken by the author except the photograph on page 69, which was taken by Meghan Duffey.

Check out our Web Site   http://www.ghoststories.com

First printing 1997.

Cover: The water color drawing of "The Homestead" was specifically designed by the internationally renouned artist, Stan Joel Strickland. (see story on page 73)

Cover design by Maryanne May.

Library of Congress Cataloging-in-Publication Data

Duffey, Barbara, 1943-

Angels and Apparitions: True Ghost Stories from the South/
Barbara Duffey.

Includes bibliographical references.
ISBN 0-9659477-0-X (pbk.)
1. Angels. 2. Ghosts—South. 3. Apparitions, American—South.
4. Supernatural phenomena. I. Title.

CIP: 97-061412

ACKNOWLEDGMENTS

This book would not have been possible without the generosity of all the people who graciously donated their experiences and stories. These people are true believers in the supernatural and hope that their personal accounts will in some way help others to understand that death is not the end and that the soul is immortal.

We don't understand why these spiritual phenomena happen to some people and not others or why they occur at all. We can only pay tribute to the stories and acknowledge that they are true and not the magnification of imaginations.

This book is truly made possible by the support of my husband, Jeff Duffey, and my daughter, Meghan Duffey, who have tirelessly accompanied me all over the South to investigate the leads that I received.

I would like to extend a special thank you to Judy Vickers who spent hours editing the manuscript and added her expertise in many areas. I would also like to thank Deana Burgess for her efforts in proofreading the final draft. Without the generosity of all these people this book could not have been written.

TABLE OF CONTENTS

DEDICATION

*I dedicate this book to my husband, Jeff,
my three children, Andrew, Matthew, and Meghan,
and the power of the Holy Spirit.*

LOUISIANA

DESTREHAN PLANTATION

DESTREHAN PLANTATION
DESTREHAN, LOUISIANA

Are the restless ghosts of the two-hundred-year-old Destrehan Plantation plaguing visitors and tour guides in hopes of revealing the truth and anguish that occurred there over a century ago? Some think so and feel compelled to pursue the answers to the long hidden secrets, while others deny any existence of ghost activity or ever witnessing the presence of visitors from the past.

Madeline Levatino, once a tour guide and author of the book *Past Masters: The History and Hauntings of Destrehan Plantation*, still seeks to discover the truth and claims that she receives messages from time to time from the spirits. Perhaps they are trying to avenge their untimely deaths or merely set the record straight. Whatever the reason, visitors still witness the apparition of a young girl wearing a beige dress with a lace collar, playing in the playroom. Others have seen the form of a man dressed in the clothing of the early 1800s. Once a psychic writer drew the attention of several spirit souls who couldn't wait to speak through her. Madeline thinks that the spirits won't rest until the tragedies of their past lives have been exposed and the truth told once and for all.

The magnificent plantation on the river road was built by French settler Robert Antoine Robin de Logny in 1787. After amassing a small fortune and marrying Jeanne Dreux, the daughter of a wealthy land owner, Robin de Logny purchased the large tract of indigo-producing land twenty-five miles north of New

Orleans, fronting the Mississippi River. He contracted with a master builder named Charles, a free man of color, to construct a mansion that would benefit his wealthy station in life and provide an ample home for his wife and four children. It took three years to build the original structure with the help of a few slaves. But, unfortunately, Robin de Logny died in 1792, only two years after his dream plantation home was completed. Robin de Logny had no way of knowing then that his mansion would survive and be protected as part of a National Historical Trust two hundred years later and that his creole decedents would distinguish themselves as members of the first families of Louisiana both in wealth and political service.

In 1786 Robin de Logny's youngest daughter, Marie Claude Celeste, married the wealthy and distinguished Jean Noel Destrehan, the creole son of noble ancestry. (*Creole* means first generation born in Louisiana from French or German parents.) After the death of Robin de Logny, Jean Noel Destrehan bought the plantation in St. Charles Parish for his wife, and over the years it became known as Destrehan Plantation. Together they raised fourteen children. As a true Catholic family, they were very religious and held services often; the parish priest was in constant attendance to the family, their visitors and slaves.

In 1811 the largest slave uprising ever recorded in the history of the United States occurred thirty miles north of New Orleans, lasted for three days and ended at Destrehan Plantation. Approximately two hundred slaves from the neighboring plantations marched on the levee toward New Orleans, killing two land owners, wounding others and burning property as they went. Governor William C. Claiborne dispatched two companies of militia headed by General Wade Hampton, U. S. commander-in-chief of the Southern Forces, to quickly overcome the insurrection. A bloodbath resulted when all the slaves but twenty-one were killed in combat. Afterwards, a short trial was held on Destrehan Plantation, and the other slaves were sent back to their own plantations to be executed. Two slaves from Destrehan were found guilty and also hanged.

Jean Noel Destrehan became interested in politics and in 1812 was elected the first United States Senator from Louisiana. But he declined the office to remain in Louisiana as a state senator, not wanting to spend so much time away from his home and family. Working with his brother-in-law, Etienne de Bore, who pioneered in developing the process of granulating sugar from sugar cane, Destrehan converted his plantation from growing indigo to cultivating the tall grass crops producing sugar cane. This conversion to sugar cane reaped him great profits, and de Bore eventually amassed one of the largest fortunes ever bequeathed in Louisiana History.

All his life Jean Noel Destrehan was loved and respected by his fellow Louisianans. He was a very modest man who lived simply, well below the grand style his fortune might support. But the question that has never been answered is why he bequeathed his young, beautiful and talented daughter, Elinore Zelia Destrehan in marriage to a virtual newcomer to the area. The Scottish born immigrant Steven Henderson, a man twice her age, was not a creole and had no social position in the community. His only claim to fame was his vast fortune, which he mysteriously accumulated, almost overnight, some say from slave trade.

Zelia and Henderson were married on October 19, 1816, when she was only sixteen years old and he a man of 40. Shortly after their marriage, Destrehan Plantation, which had been for sale, passed into Steven Henderson's hands. There are no bills of sale on record confirming this transaction. Zelia never bore any children, and it was rumored that she lived a difficult life. Steven Henderson had a reputation of being a very brutal task master to his slaves, and some even called him evil.

Zelia left Destrehan Plantation, some say for good, in her late twenties to live in New York. She never returned and ultimately died in New York of unknown causes on September 19, 1830. Her last will and testament named her husband as sole heir to her fortune, excluding her sisters and brothers. She mentioned that she dictated this document of her own free will and was not forced. Six years later her brother, Rene, who had lived at Destrehan for many years with Zelia, was found dead in a New York hotel, reportedly of unknown causes. Perhaps they had both contracted a secret disease and traveled to New York for treatment. The death records do not reveal the truth. Or maybe they were both assisted in their untimely deaths by the direction of Mr. Henderson. Whatever happened still remains a mystery.

After Steven Henderson died two years later, the plantation was bought from his only heir, a Henderson nephew, by Zelia's sister, Louise Odile, and her husband, Judge Rost, executor to Henderson's estate, for a fair market value. Once again the plantation returned to the family. They immediately began the much needed improvements and additions to the house in the Greek Revival style of architecture. The cypress columns were enclosed with immense Doric columns. The back gallery was completely enclosed, creating a foyer on the plantation side of the house. The high ceilings were closed in, plastered over and decorated with huge carved medallions suitable to the Greek Revival style of the day. The doors were decorated with elaborate keyhole-style wood moldings. At the foyer's entry two magnificent winding staircases were carved out of cypress and black walnut, adding southern charm and dignity to the once plain large home. Under the direction of Judge Rost, by 1854 the plantation became once again the largest producer of sugar cane and corn in St. Charles Parish. The Rosts received and were entertained by the most wealthy families of the time.

At the beginning of the War Between the States, Judge Rost was appointed Minister to France by Jefferson Davis, the President of the Confederacy, and proceeded to Paris immediately with his family to entice French financial support for the Confederacy.

In 1862 the plantation was confiscated by Union troops along with all Rost's other land holdings and commandeered under the command of General Nathaniel Banks, who converted the home into one of the Freedman's Bureaus. It was held in enemy hands until the end of the war. When Judge Rost returned in 1866, all his personal holdings were eventually returned to him. Unfortunately, Judge Rost died two years later, leaving his wife and children alone to manage his vast fortune and properties.

In 1877, Emile Rost, the Judge's youngest son, bought all the rights of ownership to the plantation when his mother died. He was the last member of the Destrehan family to own the plantation. In 1910 he sold out to commercial sugar producers, ending 123 years of family ownership.

APPARITIONS AND OTHER HAUNTINGS
ON DESTREHAN PLANTATION

According to reports in a November 4, 1984, *Times-Picayune* newspaper article by Kristen Gilger, "Manor Spirits Awake," the apparition of a tall, dark man made a number of appearances in 1980, and the witnesses claimed that he might be the pirate Jean Lafitte, searching for his lost treasures. During the late 1700s there had been rumors that the pirate kept a boat moored in a small canal on Destrehan Plantation with the permission of the owner, but no one knows for sure. Perhaps the original owner, Robin de Logny, had become good friends with the pirate; maybe they even financed joint ventures as was common in that time.

This is only speculation, however.

In 1984 the administrator Joan Douville claimed that the renovations and excavations must have shaken loose and aroused the spirits because craftsmen working on the mansion reported half a dozen sightings. This time the apparition of a man dressed in an 1830s white suit with wide lapels and a white cornered hat appeared to several family members of the assistant administrator Jolene Roper. On another occasion a visitor to the mansion saw the same ghost near the wrought iron gates that separate the plantation from the river road. Ms. Douville, originally a skeptic, confessed to seeing him one dreary afternoon in the second floor room once used as a nursery.

Mrs. Roper's nineteen-year-old daughter experienced a very strange phenomenon. She was in bed late one night when she heard footsteps outside her door. She called to her parents, but no one answered. Then she witnessed the apparition of a man coming into her room. Too scared to watch, she turned away and waited, hoping the form would disappear. When she turned back, he had not vanished as she had hoped, but sat silently by her bed. Only his head and upper chest were visible, resembling a dense white cloud. She felt his strong presence, which frightened her, but she occasionally ran her hand through him to see if she could send him away, but he didn't move. He remained there until about 5:30 in the morning just staring at her. When her dad turned on a light, the apparition disappeared without a trace.

She sensed his presence twice after that first sighting. The same thing happened. Annette was sure someone was standing near her, and when she turned around to see, the ghost appeared. Again the man said nothing, but continued to look at her. Later, while examining pictures from the Destrehan family collection, Annette concluded that the apparition must have been Steven Henderson, the man who married Zelia, Jean Noel Destrehan's sixteen-year-old daughter. Often Annette was told that she strongly resembled a picture they found of Zelia. Some speculated that this was the reason that Steven Henderson's ghost seemed to be obsessed with Annette.

Spirit Activity at Destrehan

Rumors of ghost sightings were not new at Destrehan because over the years many different spirit phenomena have been reported. Police and local residents have often seen a strange glow of light on the gallery or coming from a window when all else was dark. Psychics and other visitors have seen spirits in almost every room of the mansion, while others have witnessed hot and cold spots, unexplained footsteps and other strange noises.

Strange faces have appeared in photographs taken by visitors to Destrehan after the film was developed, faces that had not been visible when the photo was taken.

Madeline Levatino

Madeline had worked at Destrehan for only a week as a tour guide when she felt a terrible "cold" spot on one of the great winding stairs. Along with the cold came a deep foreboding and a sense that the walls and ceilings were shouting, "Get out!" She knew an invisible presence was standing at the opposite end of the hall, but she was afraid to turn around. She took this activity as a stern warning, but she didn't know why at the time.

Jean Noel Destrehan Sighted

In the mid 1980s Phyllis Barraco worked in the gift shop which was located in the downriver wing of the mansion. A female visitor asked her if there had ever been any strange ghost activity in the house. After Phyllis mentioned that a distinguished man with hair graying at the temples, long sideburns and a heavy French accent had been seen several times, the woman announced that she had just spoken with him. She thought he was rather strange because he wore a heavy black coat that seemed unseasonably warm for the extreme heat wave in the area at the time. When Phyllis showed her a picture of Jean Noel Destrehan, the woman agreed that he was the man she had just observed, standing on the gallery.

In a thick French accent, the man asked her why she had come to visit Destrehan Plantation. The woman confessed that she was researching her genealogy and thought that a distant relative had lived here as a slave. When she gave the man the slave's name, he immediately shook his head and assured her that no one by that name had ever worked on Destrehan. At the time, she questioned how this stranger would know this information, but before she could ask him anything else, he said that he hoped she would find what she was looking for. Then he quickly joined a tour group passing down the hall.

After Phyllis heard this story, she decided to investigate on her own. She closed the shop and proceeded to where she thought the tour group had gone after the encounter. When she found them, the man described was not among the other visitors, and the guide denied ever seeing anyone resembling the man's description.

THE AUTOMATIC WRITER

One Sunday afternoon in 1993, a man who claimed to be psychic and to have the ability to receive messages from spirits joined the tour group. When he reached the stairs to the attic, he became very nervous and anxious, saying that strong negative vibrations were coming from the attic.

"He wants me to leave," said the psychic.

Madeline, the tour guide, asked him if he could see anything. The psychic answered that he saw a dark-haired man standing in the attic who was about six-feet-one or -two inches tall and wearing a large black cape.

Madeline knew immediately that the spirit was Nicolas Noel Destrehan, the son of Jean Noel Destrehan. He had been described to her as a one-armed man who always wore a large black cape. He had lost his arm in a machine accident.

The psychic felt more positive about the sighting and appeared to relax more. He said the spirit was sitting on a beam and wore tight pants and black leather boots.

"Two little girls are joining him," the psychic said. "One is tall and dark, and the other who seems a little younger has lighter hair. She's wearing a white or beige dress with a dark vest. He says your ideas about the girls are wrong."

Madeline was surprised to hear this because she had been researching the identity of the two young girl ghosts, who had been seen by many visitors to Destrehan. Until that moment, she thought she had discovered their identity.

Madeline and the psychic returned to the gift shop. The psychic confessed that he had seen quite a few spirits, both black and white, appear to him from the opening of the attic. He wanted a pencil and paper because, he confessed, they all had something to say.

The man began recording immediately in French and English what the spirits said:

"Many dwell here, black and white. The black woman grieves for her son who died at ten years in 1840 or 41. This may be verified by checking the records."

When the psychic was shown a picture of Nicolas, he exclaimed that the man in the attic was, indeed, the same man. The likeness was identical. He also said the spirit had two arms and at one point acted playful by extending his arm deliberately and seemed to produce the two ghost girls on demand. As he did so, Nicolas laughed out loud.

The psychic, pencil and paper in hand, decided to walk outside around the grounds of the mansion to see what other information he could pick up.

When he returned to the gift shop, he produced a drawing for the tour guides that resembled a dark woman wearing a turban wrapped around her hair. The woman was crying, and both her arms were stretched out in grief. He had written the following message from her:

> She grieves for her son. She repeats "porquoi Gaston?" She wanted he (sic) to become a priest. She's saying he didn't belong being caught up in this "insanity."
> She cannot leave. She knows all. The kind master was replaced by the devel (sic). "Gaston" repeated.

The tour guides realized that a message similar to this one had been reported by another visitor more than a year before. The person communicating the message also saw the turbaned woman.

Madeline begged the psychic to return to the attic and copy the messages that came from the spirits there. The psychic was very tired but reluctantly agreed. When he returned, the messages were written in Old French, which was transcribed into the following:

"We don't like the lights.
The slaves toujours
dreamed of successful overthrow
of the masters . . .
"Beauregard was treated
as royalty here. The evil one
kept his vile deeds secret.
"Those who come here
to decipher the truth
must be extremely wary as one
perpetrates great lies,
"J'ai le main maintenant.
"You and others have penetrated
the veil. Madeline wants a
messagge. Tres bien. Tell her
I know full well how much
she wrestled within before she came
out on the side of our existence.
"Extinguish these lights as they
frighten us. Candlelight
would fare better.
"Know well I am not the evil one.
Yes, the Welshman (not true
Scotsman) lies all too well.
"The black woman speaks the truth.
She has seen the crucifix
replaced late at night by the altar
to Satan. The death of her
beloved garcon is related to this.
So sad. He was a true child of God
and deserved not his tragic fate.
"Adieu mon ami.
Tell Madeleine to persevere
in proving our reality."
—Pierre

Madeline discovered that Pierre was listed among the slaves of Robin de Logny, Jean Noel Destrehan and Steven Henderson, until 1838, when his name did not appear any longer. Madeline is still trying to discover the truth. Perhaps this man was involved in the slave uprising in 1811. Perhaps Pierre was one of the slaves to be freed by Henderson's will, which stipulated that all his slaves be given their freedom. But the executor, Judge Rost, defied that request and obtained a court order mandating that the slaves remain as part of Henderson's estate, which he promptly purchased on April 11, 1839. Perhaps Pierre was freed, and that's why his name didn't appear on the slave lists after that date. No one will ever know the whole truth, but Madeline is still trying to unravel some of the dark mysteries.

Since the visit by the psychic, "the lights" in the attic were eventually turned off at night. No one knew that the main breaker did not disconnect these lights.

Madeline is still researching the lives of the owners of Destrehan; for some unknown reason, she feels compelled to do so. On October 20, 1990, Madeline Levatino's wedding day, the image of a spirit appeared in a photograph taken of Madeline with her bridesmaid. Madeline and her bridesmaid were facing a lovely, antique oval full length floor mirror, and the photograph was to be of their reflection. When the photo was developed, another image appeared in the photo. The face was covered by a veil, but its hazy image appeared to be standing behind the reflections of Madeline and her bridesmaid.

It appears that the ghosts at Destrehan are still in a state of unrest, but even though there have been many sightings, the spirits have been harmless. Perhaps they are the ones responsible for maintaining a prevailing feeling of peace that one feels while touring the mansion.

In 1971 the Amoco Oil Company donated the house at

Destrehan Plantation to the River Road Historical Society, a nonprofit organization. Because of the diligent efforts of faithful volunteers, the house was saved from neglect and certain destruction. They supervised its careful restoration and acquired furnishings appropriate for its once 1840s elegance. Over the years the Amoco Oil Company has remained a generous contributor to the continuing maintenance and restoration of the house. It is now open to the public seven days a week.

THE LALAURIE HOUSE

THE LALAURIE HOUSE
THE FRENCH QUARTER
NEW ORLEANS, LOUISIANA

In the immutable French Quarter in New Orleans, Louisiana, resides the renowned Lalaurie House, an elegant three-story brick and stucco mansion which has marked the corner of Royal and Gov. Nicholls Streets since 1825. For over a century, tales have shrouded the historic landmark with tragedy and intrigue. The mansion was named for the first owner, Madam Lalaurie, who with her French physician husband distinguished the mansion by hosting flamboyant social gatherings, elaborate balls and extravagant galas. But there is also a dark side; they blackened the reputation of the house by abusing their slaves and, some say, even torturing them to death.

According to reports in the New Orleans *Times Picayune*, November 12, 1988, strange noises originate from the slave quarters on dreary, storm-ridden nights. Some say that the clanking of slave chains and the searing whine of a leather whip reverberate in the courtyard. No live individual has ever been discovered causing the mysterious clamor.

This distinguished mansion's 9,000 square-foot living area includes the most elaborately decorated marble-floored double parlors and a French ballroom which was extensively plastered with scroll work, flower designs and then gilded in gold leaf. The narrow 46 by 90 foot lot also includes a four-story back wing, which houses the accommodations for staff and guests. This area was once used as the slave quarters.

The fifteen-room mansion has only four bedrooms, but each is embellished with richly carved molding and imported marble fireplaces. On clear days the widow's walk towering above the roof, a cupola, allows access to a complete view of the French Quarter and the Mississippi River beyond. In 1988 the house was offered for sale for $1.9 million dollars.

During its early history the mansion was blackened by smoke from a fierce fire. Neighbors frantically trying to douse the flames were stunned to discover seven slaves chained to the wall and suffering in various degrees of starvation and torment. The Lalauries were so humiliated and ridiculed by the discovery that they were forced to leave and quickly escaped to Paris.

Ever since that tragic day, the residents of New Orleans claim that the spirits of other tortured slaves haunt the house and will never leave it in peace. Many have reported seeing dark, shadowy figures flitting from window to doorway. Others have heard mysterious, hoarse voices when no one else was around. The clanking of the slave's chains and the cracking of a whip still clearly echo in the halls and are heard by those who dare to visit the house on dark nights.

MISSISSIPPI

THE GHOSTS OF ROWAN OAK
1840
WILLIAM FAULKNER'S HOME
OXFORD, MISSISSIPPI

The spirit of William Faulkner, the great American author who won the Nobel Prize in literature in 1949, still lingers in the small town of Oxford, Mississippi. I don't know if this perception emanates from the lasting power of his tragic characters and the reminder that Oxford is the location of their origin or if the illusion is from the aura of the man himself. But when I crossed the boundary of his farm at the end of a city road, I knew I hadn't been fooled. His presence permeated the air like a cool fog on a fall morning. It seemed to move with me as I crossed the damp black earth under the wisteria vines, and I sensed it again as I walked through the gate from his barn and paddock to head toward the house. I felt his spirit again as I stood on a small hidden patio at the edge of the lawn. I imagined him, laughing and drinking there with several of his friends, and in another vision, I saw the troubled writer obsessing over an unfinished scene, sitting there, alone, in anguish, with his alcohol, trying to put his feelings and words on paper.

His only daughter, Jill Faulkner Summers, often said that her "Pappy" could be most reluctant with adults, but had a world of patience with children. At Halloween he often told the children the story about Judith Sheegog, the ghost of his Rowan Oak home.

When the Yankees came through Oxford during the War Between the States, Judith fell in love with a Union soldier. But

ROWAN OAK

soon the soldiers left, and Judith became inconsolable. She was so distraught that she jumped from the Rowan Oak balcony and fell to her death. People say she would have died of a broken heart if she hadn't committed suicide.

Because of her suicide, she wasn't permitted a Christian burial in the town cemetery. Her family laid her body to rest under the largest magnolia tree at Rowan Oak.

On Halloween Faulkner recounted the story and took children to the tree to try to summon her spirit. According to all reports, however, she never appeared.

Tour guides frequently tell this story to the groups of people from all over the world who visit Rowan Oak every year. When questioned about other ghosts there, the tour guides were very open. One said that occasionally when he comes to work and first enters the house, he hears the sound of a piano playing. Others have heard the sounds of children laughing and of footsteps on the second floor.

According to an article in the *National Geographic Magazine*, when Faulkner's niece spent the night in the house, she was awakened suddenly by an aroma like that of her uncle's burning pipe tobacco. She knew immediately that his ghost was right there in the room with her.

During Faulkner's life, Rowan Oak was not only his home, but his refuge from the stresses of the outside world. He retreated there like a bear to his den, to contemplate the struggles and melancholy of the people he met. His characters live on, and, having withstood the test of time, they are considered classic among others in the field of literature around the world.

Since Rowan Oak is considered a historic site and is open to the public, it will always remain just as Faulkner left it, pristine in its peace, a tiny spot in the universe where his spirit can still roam free and meditate.

BEAUVOIR

BEAUVOIR
BILOXI, MISSISSIPPI

Jefferson Davis, the president of the Confederacy, spent his last years at Beauvoir writing his memoirs: *The Rise and Fall of the Confederate Government.* In 1877 he rented the east cottage called the Pavilion from an old friend, Mrs. Dorsey, and used this small guest house as his office, library and bedroom. In April of 1878 Mrs. Davis joined him at Beauvoir and for the next three years assisted him in writing his manuscript in longhand. When the Davises lived at Beauvoir, it was the social center of the South, and by the second year of his stay, Davis bought the house from Mrs. Dorsey for $5,500. Mrs. Dorsey died before Davis's mortgage was paid, but she forgave his debt and left the house and acreage to him in her will. In 1889 Davis became deathly ill while on a business trip to his old plantation at Brierfield, in Warren County, Mississippi. Davis was never able to return to Beauvoir and died in New Orleans. Four years later his remains were moved to Richmond, Virginia.

The Davises suffered devastation both financially and emotionally during the reconstruction period after the war just as their fellow Southerners did. Having lost their fortune, they were dependent on family and friends for survival. Their only maiden daughter Winnie (Varina Anne Davis) fell in love with a prosperous Northerner from New York. The relationship caused so much discontent among their friends and relatives that Winnie gave up her prospects of marrying and spent most of her years at her father's side. Later, after his death, both Winnie and her mother moved to New York City. After again refusing to marry, Winnie died a maiden lady in 1898 at Narragansett Pier.

The Davises donated Beauvoir to homeless veterans of the Confederacy as a home and hospital until 1903 when Mrs. Davis sold it to the Mississippi Division of the Sons of Confederate Veterans. Twelve dormitories, a hospital, a chapel and a few cottages were erected as part of the home. In the cemetery behind Beauvoir, over 1,000 Confederate soldiers find their place of rest. These were men who followed Jefferson Davis through the war, and some of the graves belong to the veterans who lived out their years at Beauvoir.

The soft breezes from the Gulf of Mexico still cool the lovely planters style home just as they did in 1877, and the white sand beaches stretch as far as the eye can see to the east and to the west. When standing there on the shaded lawn of Beauvoir, one can surely say that this point of land marks the end of the Confederate States because to the south there lies only a vast ocean.

There are spirits at Beauvoir, too. The spirit of the South is still embodied by the Sons of Confederate Veterans, their families and supporters. These people are not a rebellious sort, but merely a group of men who love history, love their family and love the South. Their mission is not to forget the War Between the States and the truth behind the battles that ripped the South apart. There is dissension there, too. The sense of tragedy is not lost in the atmosphere; the melancholy sense of defeat permeates the air, the earth and even the soft ocean breeze. Perhaps this is why Mrs. Davis and Winnie left Beauvoir for New York; they couldn't bear to see the new face of the South.

According to some reports there is a ghost there, too, in the guest house. It seems to be some kind of poltergeist who returns occasionally to make himself known. No one knows who the

THE PAVILION

spirit is, but he creates tremendous noises that sound as if someone is crashing into the glass cases that contain the priceless mementoes from the South's First Family. Late in the afternoon visitors hear the sounds of glass breaking and go running to see what happened. No one is ever found to have caused the clamor, and no glass is ever found broken. The Davises were such nonviolent people when they were alive that no one thinks it could be them. Perhaps it is the spirit of some lone, angry Confederate, still wanting to rain havoc with his revenge. But on second thought, it could be the spirit of the late Jefferson Davis wanting to be freed from the confines of his grave.

Beauvoir is open to the public daily.

THE TWISTED OAKS OF BILOXI
BILOXI, MISSISSIPPI

In the churchyard of the old Episcopal Church in Biloxi, there were two twisted old moss-draped live oak trees that had the appearance of being tied together in a knot near the middle. For over a century there was a legend associated with those trees.

An Indian chief had a daughter who was the fairest of all the young maidens. A young warrior sought to marry the beautiful girl, but the chief refused because he disliked the young brave. Finally, after many refusals of many gifts offered in the honor of the girl, the chief finally declared, "When two mighty oaks become tied together in one inseparable knot only then will I give my consent."

The brave went away in great sorrow and black despair. His soul was dying at the thought of living life without his true love. But he was not alone in his pleadings. His entire village sent up prayers to the Gods, hoping for favor in this brave's case. Before long, a storm gathered on the horizon, and soon it became a storm the likes of which no one had ever seen. The storm broke with such force that it destroyed everything in sight, including the Indian village.

The next morning all that was left standing in the village were two huge oaks that had been torn and twisted together in the form of a knot. When the Indian chief saw this, he ordered the marriage immediately. The brave and the Indian princess lived happily ever after.

MCRAVEN
VICKSBURG, MISSISSIPPI

The ghosts at McRaven aren't shy, says Leyland French, owner-operator and guide to the antebellum mansion located in downtown Vicksburg. He refers to it as the most haunted house in all of Mississippi and boasts that it has been written about many times. But he assures his guests that the ghosts are kind and not to be feared.

History is still visible at McRaven, not only from the appearance of its ghosts, but displayed in the architectural changes found in each new addition. The first section of the mansion was built in 1797 in the Frontier cottage style of architecture. The galleried second section, built in 1836, reflects the Louisiana charm of the Creole influence. By 1849, though, the Greek Revival style had infiltrated all the other types of architecture throughout the South, and McRaven's final addition copied the other plantation mansions with their spacious verandas and galleries.

During the Battle of Vicksburg, McRaven was in the center of the action. The Union Navy attacked Vicksburg from the Mississippi River for almost fourteen months and fired more than 22,000 shells into the town. The Union Army also poured into the town an estimated 2,800 shells a day for 47 days. Few of the citizens were killed because they hid themselves in cellars and deep caves they dug underneath the city. Living the meagerest of existences, the citizens ate mule meat and drank from mudholes. Pounds of bullets and shell fragments have been recovered from

McRaven by previous owners. During the renovations many of
the battlescars were removed, but some scars were allowed to
remain in the hall and parlor as mementoes of a terrible experience.

On the 4th of July in 1995, during a reenactment of the Battle
of Vicksburg and holiday celebration, more than fifty reenactors,
their wives and children camped around the mansion and received
the thrill of their lives. They watched in awe as a man dressed in
a Confederate uniform walked back and forth across an invisible
gallery on the south side of the house. They didn't understand
why he was walking in the air until they learned that the original
mansion had identical galleries on both the front and back of the
house, but during the War the gallery in the back burned and was
never replaced. The man paraded along this "invisible" gallery
and disappeared as mysteriously as he appeared.

During that same weekend while tourists were walking past
the parlor, a child ran up and touched the middle c key on the
antique piano, but nothing happened. Mr. French assured her
that the piano was in perfect working order, and with that comment
the instrument began to play on its own and filled the house with
a lovely melody. All the tourists were amazed by such a display
of supernatural activity. Of course, Mr. French is as surprised by
the ghost activity as anyone else.

On another occasion a tour guide witnessed a lamp rise up
in the air, turn on its side and return gently to the table.

Mississippi college professor Charles Sullivan spent the night
in the house before his Civil-War style wedding at McRaven and
reported:

> "The house is genuinely haunted. There are things not of
> this mortal world there. Sounds, sights and definitely
> something that wants the lights in one particular bedroom
> left on."

He didn't sleep at all during the night at McRaven because "the chandelier kept lighting up." Every time he turned the light switch to "off," it turned itself back to "on" again. Sullivan said he spent the long night in "a solid state of high nervous tension" behind the old-style mosquito netting of his antique canopy bed.

Others have had similar experiences says the owner Mr. French. Some have claimed sighting an attractive brown-haired woman in a distinctive brown gown looking out at them from various windows of the three-story house. French has not only identified the gown as "definitely in the 1830s creation," but he also says that he knows the wearer to be Mary Elizabeth Howard, the lady who inspired her husband to build the mansion a century and a half ago.

The room Sullivan slept in belonged to Elizabeth, and over the years this is the room where the lights are often turned on without warning. Some say that she always liked to keep it as brightly lit as possible. "She just hasn't been able to leave McRaven," French said. Perhaps she was afraid of the dark, and her spirit still is.

McRaven still stands today in its great magnificence as a reminder of what the Old South must have been like. But this longevity was not without a price. After the South's surrender in 1865, the town of Vicksburg was inhabited by Yankee troops.

John Bobb, the owner of McRaven at that time, so angered the troops that they shot and killed him in his garden. Anxious to rectify a desperate situation, General Grant court-martialed the guilty men, and they were later hanged.

No one knows for sure who the ghosts at McRaven are or when they will appear in the future. But one thing is certain: the spirits loved the home so much that they have been reluctant to leave, and because of Mr. French's good nature, they feel comfortable enough to appear frequently.

A UNION SOLDIER CALLS FROM HIS GRAVE
VICKSBURG, MISSISSIPPI

Mr. and Mrs. David Connoly tried to ignore a psychic's plea. The couple met a strange woman who called herself a psychic at a party one night in New Orleans. After speaking with her for only a short time, the psychic told them things about their life that they didn't think anyone else could have known. The psychic did not stop there. She confessed that she had strong feelings that they would be moving north to a house once owned by Mr. Connoly's relative, a man who had been a Union prisoner of war in the Confederate prison, Andersonville, in Georgia. His ghost was still caught in some sort of time energy warp and couldn't leave until they brought a possession owned by his mother to the ghost's house. The psychic's premonition seemed strange to the Connolys, especially when they never intended to move.

But the Connolys couldn't forget about the odd prediction and decided to investigate. When discussing the information with Mr. Connoly's family, his mother admitted that two brothers had been prisoners of war at Andersonville. One had escaped, and the last the family heard was that he had reached the Mississippi River, where they lost contact with him.

Not long after the psychic incident transpired, the Connolys were forced to move to Vicksburg, Mississippi, because of business. They purchased a dilapidated antebellum house supposedly used as nurses' quarters during the War Between the States. When they were cleaning out the attic, they discovered records hidden in a box of old books that had belonged to previous owners. They were hoping to find information about the original structure of the house. Much to their surprise, they recognized one of the previous owner's names. After the war the house had been purchased by Mr. Connoly's lost relative, a great uncle, the soldier who had escaped from Andersonville.

Over the years, the Connolys saw the spirit of his great uncle walking through the house. Sometimes they saw a shadowy figure cross the hall as the sun was setting over the Mississippi. Mrs. Connoly said that the spirit stopped its appearances when her mother-in-law moved into the house. The woman brought a pair of brass candlesticks belonging to her family and placed them on the mantle in the living room. Ever since that time, it seemed as if the ghost activity stopped. But when the candle sticks were moved to another room, the activity started again.

People have seen men standing like sentry's at the edge of the Connoly's property. Voices in the hall, steps on the stairs, and banging noises often kept even the most sound sleeper awake at night. The Connolys just accepted the activity as part of the house's charm and individuality.

In the 1990s Mrs. Connoly gave up trying to improve the property because the carpenters always quit. They kept hearing noises. One morning when Mrs. Connoly was standing under a mimosa tree, she heard a voice say, "Good Morning." She said, "Good Morning," in return, and then the carpenter said, "Good Morning." That's the closest Mrs. Connoly has come to speaking to the garbled voices that followed her around the house.

GEORGIA

BARNSLEY GARDENS

BARNSLEY GARDENS AND ETERNAL LOVE
ADAIRSVILLE, GEORGIA

In 1824 when Godfrey Barnsley was eighteen years of age, he arrived on American soil with only four shillings in his pocket. In ten years time, he had become one of the wealthiest men in Georgia by marketing American cotton to the English cloth mills. He established offices in Savannah, New York, New Orleans and Liverpool, and his ships exported goods like cotton, salt, wine and carpeting all over the world.

After creating his fortune, Godfrey courted Julia Henrietta Scarborough, the daughter of one of Savannah's richest men, a blond-haired, blue-eyed beauty who was bright and very accomplished for the day. Her father, William Scarborough, II, was a prosperous shipping merchant and was instrumental in building the first steamship to cross the Atlantic. Julia's mother wasn't in favor of the match but was forced to relinquish her daughter's hand in marriage anyway. From Julia and Godfrey's first meeting, their love proved to be a strong enough force to sway the doubts and misgivings Julia's parents had about this union.

After Godfrey and Julia were married in 1828, they moved to England for two years where their first child, Anna, was born. But Godfrey's business forced him to travel to New York and Savannah, leaving Julia terribly lonely, so they moved back to her home in Savannah. By 1838 Julia had given birth to six children: Anna, Reginald, who died at two and a half years, Harold, Adelaide, Julia and George. But Julia's health declined after so many births, and she suffered from consumption or what we now call tuberculosis.

Godfrey desperately wanted to get Julia and his children away from the tainted Savannah air. So in 1840 he bought 3,600 acres of land that had been part of the Cherokee Nation in Bartow County, Georgia. He soon cleared the forests to make way for the construction of his immense "manor" home. But Godfrey didn't know that a Cherokee chief had put a curse on the land, claiming that it had been sacred to the Cherokee nation and contained some burial mounds.

When Godfrey brought his wife Julia and their six children, including Lucien, the new baby, to North Georgia to live, they were housed in a crude log cabin until the manor home could be built.

Business still drew Godfrey away from his family for eight to ten months at a time almost every year. Julia continued to grow very lonely and found frontier life difficult, but she fell in love with their new Italian "manor" home and named it Woodlands. Godfrey wanted its gardens to become an example of horticultural excellence that would rival the gardens of Europe.

By 1844 Julia's health had declined. After her son Lucien died at eighteen months of age, she wrote in a letter to her children who were away at school that she was so sick she couldn't answer their letters, but she still loved them more than she could say. Soon after, she was rushed to Savannah by train to be attended by her childhood physician, but she died there in February, 1845.

Godfrey was overcome with grief over the loss of his precious Julia. With the help of a governess, Julia's mother cared for the children in Godfrey's absence, but they all missed their mother and father deeply.

Godfrey could not bear to go home to Woodlands, where he felt Julia's absence more than anywhere else. During a visit to

THE BOXWOOD PARTERRE

Mobile, Alabama, however, Godfrey participated in a seance with
a psychic and was told he could communicate with his dead wife.
The psychic told him that spirits will return to the place they
loved most and that he was sure to find Julia at Woodlands.

Godfrey's mourning of Julia ended when he began to
communicate with Julia's spirit in the boxwood parterre near the
fountain on their woodland estate. One of the carpenters claimed
that Godfrey often remarked to him that Julia had suggested a
specific idea the previous night. The carpenter didn't question
Mr. Barnsley, only carried out his requests. He claimed that
Godfrey mentioned that he spoke to Julia around the fountain in
the boxwood. The carpenter also added that Mr. Barnsley
appeared most content when walking through his gardens.
Godfrey and Julia's love had broken all boundaries and had proved
that love is truly eternal.

During the prosperous years before the War Between the
States, Godfrey traveled extensively and always returned with
elegant and priceless furnishings, including millwork, for his

Woodlands Manor home. He claimed that Julia advised his purchases and directed the planting of his precious, rare imported roses, trees and other plants. Experts say that his Chinese Fir is the largest specimen of its kind in the United States. Some say that his mansion, furnished with flushing toilets and both hot and cold running water, was unique for its time.

The family's years were not without tragedy, even with the presence of Julia's spirit. In 1856 Godfrey's son, Harold, disappeared with a ship bound for the Orient. Some said he was attacked by pirates, but after an extensive search, no evidence was found. In 1858 Godfrey's daughter, Adelaide, died a week after the birth of her first child. Shortly afterwards, Godfrey suffered a tragic financial setback when the cotton market fell. It took him several years to rebuild his holdings.

In 1861 the War Between the States broke out, and Godfrey's two sons, Lucien and George, joined the Confederacy. After only a few months of active duty and participation in the battle of Manassas, George was recruited for medical school. He served out his time in the army as a doctor.

Heavy investments in the Confederacy and the devastation of war completely depleted the Barnsley fortune, and the family was left penniless. Sherman and the Yankees stripped Woodlands of all food, wine and furnishings and trampled many of the gardens except for the boxwood parterre.

For years after the war, the family struggled for the merest existence even though Godfrey traveled many times to New Orleans, trying to reestablish his cotton business there. He was unsuccessful, and in 1873, he died poor and away from his family. His daughter Julia brought him home in a copper casket to be buried at Woodlands. He would join the spirit of his beloved wife Julia, and they would finally be at rest. His son George, upset with the conditions of the South after the war, left Georgia and emigrated with some of the other Southerners to Brazil, where he established a plantation and spent the last years of his life.

Some say the Barnsley misfortune was due to the Cherokee curse; others say their misfortunes were just the effects of nature. Godfrey's daughter Julia spent her entire life and almost all of her money trying to maintain Woodlands. It seemed to be more of a burden on the family than a gift, maybe even a curse. But Godfrey and Julia were partly successful, especially in creating and preserving an eternal bond of love, and the tale of their love has been an inspiration to thousands of people for more than a century.

Godfrey's daughter, Julia, died in 1905, and shortly after her death a tornado blew the roof off the center section of the house. Julia's daughter, Addie Saylor, and her family, were forced to live in the kitchen wing, where the museum is today.

Another tragedy befell the family in 1935. Addie had two sons, Preston and Harry. Preston suffered brain damage from repeated beatings as a prize fighter in the 30s and was hospitalized in the Milledgeville Psychiatric Hospital. During one of his escapes, Preston arrived at Woodlands, his fury aimed at his brother, Harry. In the parlor of the house, Preston fired three shots at Harry. The first two bullets missed and became imbedded in the woodwork, where they remain today. The third bullet killed Harry right in front of his mother, Addie Saylor. Preston was convicted of murder and sentenced to life in prison. Blood stains still mar the floor where Harry fell.

Was this act of vengeance caused by the Cherokee curse, or was it simply the act of a demented, sick mind? No one will ever know for sure. But when Prince Frugger bought the gardens in 1988, he didn't want to take a chance. He invited the Cherokees to Barnsley Gardens and asked if they would lift the curse. Three Indian Chiefs and a medicine man prayed and blessed the land.

Immediately after their ceremony, a hawk was seen circling the ruins and then resting for a moment in the top of one of the trees. That was the first time a hawk had been seen on the place since Barnsley bought the land in the 1840s.

GHOSTS AT BARNSLEY GARDENS

Ten years after Julia's death, Godfrey received a letter from her late father, William Scarborough II:

> My dear mortal Barnsley, Julia is with me and all doing just fine.
> William Scarborough II

The signature matched perfectly that of old man Scarborough but he had been dead for ten years.

The letter is still part of the family's collection of letters.

ADDIE SAYLOR

Godfrey's granddaughter, Addie Saylor, had developed a strong belief in spiritualism over the years and even claimed that the spirit of her son, Harry, was also present in the gardens. She claimed that she had communicated with him many times, even that his ghost came to her and warned her that the Japanese were going to bomb Pearl Harbor a week before it happened. She didn't tell the government because she didn't think that anyone would listen to her.

The day of Harry's revelation, a journalist was visiting Addie, and when she told him about the warning, even though he didn't believe in ghosts, he tried to print his news in a newspaper column he wrote. Unfortunately, his editors pulled the article and refused to print it. Harry's information might have changed the course of history.

Addie also often claimed to see the spirit of her grandmother, Julia, in the garden, too. At other times she said she heard Godfrey's chair scrape across the floor in his office on the second floor, just as it always did when he was alive.

GEORGE'S GHOST

When Harry was alive, he was a skeptic and refused to believe in all the spiritualism that surrounded him. But one day he remarked that he would believe in ghosts only if one walked up to the porch and knocked on the door three times. It wasn't long before he got his wish. One rainy night in 1918, Harry and his mother heard footsteps on the front porch, followed by three knocks on the front door.

Harry got up and went to see who the visitor was. Much to his surprise and terror, his Uncle George was standing there in the doorway. As soon as Harry invited him in, George disappeared.

Later that night, the Saylors received word that their Uncle George, who was living in Brazil at the time, had died suddenly.

THE LEGEND OF THE VINES

When Prince Frugger bought Barnsley Gardens, the house ruins were covered by years of tangled, overgrown vines of honeysuckle, Virginia creeper, poison oak and others. Cutting through this mass of overgrowth took several weeks, and when the gardeners separated the vines from the brick masonry, many people claimed that blood ran out of the mortar between the bricks. Some think that it was the type of vine that produced a red juice

or dye. Others thought it was an evil omen and were frightened
by it.

Bugle Call

The tour guide Dyane Nelson remembered when the
archeologist, Gilbert Smith, examined the grounds for artifacts.
He and his partner uncovered signs of where a Union Regiment
had camped and decided to conduct an archeological dig to see
what else they might discover. After painstakingly excavating
all day and finding only a few buttons and tools, they had decided
to give up. Suddenly, they heard the sound of a bugle playing
taps in the background. They were the only people on the grounds
at the time.

Dyane Nelson also remarked that Julia could be seen in the
boxwoods every once in a while, especially when a storm was
coming. This confirms the earlier stories that Julia appears
occasionally to visitors in the garden.

Julia's Spirit Still at Barnsley

During a recent visit to Barnsley Gardens, the author attended
the Horticulture Tour of the gardens, and when the group paused
at the fountain inside the boxwoods, the author felt Julia's
presence. It was a beautiful day and musicians were playing blue
grass music on the porch of the mansion ruins. She saw a small
white cloud appear several times in the boxwood parterre at the
fountain and hover there over other groups of tourists who paused
there to hear the description of the flowers. She felt sure the
cloud was the spirit of Julia, still hovering there after more than a
century, watching over her lovely gardens.

Barnsley Gardens is open to the public every day and they welcome visitors. They have a small nursery for the sale of plants and a lovely restaurant. It is just off I-75 North, near Adairsville, one and a half hours north of Marietta. For information call (706) 773-7480.

THE 1848 HOUSE

THE 1848 HOUSE
BUSHY PARK PLANTATION
MARIETTA, GEORGIA

Dogwoods, azaleas and lush greenery greet visitors as they approach the majestic Greek Revival mansion reminiscent of the Old South. One expects Scarlett O'Hara to appear any minute. The day we were there she did appear and posed for us on the front porch. The clock seemed to have been turned back to the antebellum years of the 1850s. A soft warm breeze blew through the trees, and the sweet aroma of honeysuckle drifted on the wind from a nearby field.

The seventeen-room plantation home was completed in 1848 by Marietta's first Mayor, John H. Glover, and named "Bushy Park." Constructed of heart pine with hand-forged nails and locust wood pins, the impressive home was built to last a century. A relic from an almost forgotten era, The 1848 House is approaching its second century. The plantation's original tract of 3,000 acres represented almost all the land that now lies between Marietta and Smyrna, suburbs of Atlanta, Georgia.

No one is sure who the ghost of The 1848 House is, but many have experienced its strange antics, from the mysterious appearance of an unusually sweet perfume to the disappearance of objects.

Marietta was still a pioneer community in 1832 when the first settlers arrived. The Cherokee Indians were forced to leave in 1838, and the first railroad wasn't finished until 1850. In 1851 Mr. Glover sold the plantation to Francis H. McLeod, and after his death, his daughter, Sarah Elizabeth, and her husband, William King, lived in the home. King was the son of Georgia's founder, Roswell King.

During the War Between the States, most of the King family "refugeed" South to Savannah. Mr. King stayed behind in the mansion with all the servants and kept a diary describing the "Battle of Bushy Park":

> The firing soon commenced. I placed the servants and children for safety in the stone cellar, where I remained with them most of the time; the firing continued about half an hour while the Federal Cavalry (from Michigan) were advancing from the Powder Springs Road to our house. Many of them were killed or wounded near the house—our cavalry fell back near one o'clock, some passing over the railroad embankment, and others over Atlanta Road.

Still embedded in the wooden door frame lies a bullet from the skirmish. "Bushy Park" served as a hospital for the Union forces after the Battle, and the upstairs northwest corner bedroom was used as an operating room. Because William King had been a personal friend of General Sherman before the war, the mansion was spared the flames of the Union Army. Because of this friendship, General Sherman asked King to contact Governor Joseph E. Brown and the Confederate Vice-President, Alexander H. Stephens, to see if they would negotiate an end to the war in Georgia. Unfortunately, King's request was denied, and Georgia's fate was to end in ruin. When the Federal army left the mansion after the war, the soldiers stripped the plantation of all furnishings and valuables.

When William B. Dunaway acquired the restaurant in 1992, he became the 23rd owner of "Bushy Park." After extensive renovations he returned the decor and atmosphere of the house to that of the 1850 period and changed the name to The 1848 House. Since then the restaurant has earned the reputation of excellence for Southern Regional Cuisine.

SWEET STICKY PERFUME

Many of the waiters and waitresses have witnessed the supernatural activity occurring in the restaurant and were eager to divulge their unusual experiences. Herb Goldstein, head waiter for seven years, thinks that one of the spirits is an elderly lady:

> "Our spirit wears a sweet cologne, a sticky, sweet cologne like your grandmother would wear. We started smelling the cologne in the wine cellar at first. But now it can be smelled anywhere. When it happens we can't mistake it, because the aroma is always the same. It seems to materialize in a huge cloud, and when it appears, all the traffic in that area just stops. All the waiters and waitresses whisper to each other, 'She is here again,' stop for a second to smell the aroma and then just go on about their business."

IS THERE A POLTERGEIST AT THE 1848 HOUSE?

Other employees report finding furniture moved and glassware rearranged, sometimes even broken. They swear that when they left the restaurant the night before, everything was straight and in place. Once in a while a wine glass will fly off the shelf for no reason. One employee claimed that several times the lights flickered off and on in the sconces on one wall in the hall. When the fixture was checked by an electrician, he never could find anything wrong with the light or bulbs. Finally, one night the waiters all yelled, "George, just cut that out!" And he did. It never happened again.

The Rocking Chair

One bright, sunny afternoon in the fall of 1995, when the restaurant was rather quiet, the hostess peered out the front window to see what the weather looked like. To her amazement one of the black cane-bottomed rocking chairs on the veranda was rocking away all by itself. She called several of the other employees to the window and asked them what they saw. They all claimed to witness the same strange phenomena. The rocking chair was rocking back and forth, back and forth, without another person around or in it.

Shadows on the Stairs

Another employee remembers another episode while she was sitting upstairs in the old cloakroom. This was a small room at the top of the stairs between the two other rooms where people brought their coats; it is no longer there. Occasionally, out of the corner of her eye, she would see the shadow of a person walk up the stairs and vanish down the hall or into one of the rooms. Later, she realized that no one ever returned and that the rooms in that area of the house were always kept locked. She wondered who the visitor was, but whenever she searched that area of the house, much to her dismay, she found no one.

Missing Fruit

Just before Christmas in 1995, one of the owners was upstairs arranging a table display using fruit and a variety of evergreens. She was placing the lemons, pears and oranges in a pyramid design for a centerpiece and surrounding it with the evergreens. Before she started, she had counted out all the fruit she needed, but halfway through her arrangement, she claimed that she was missing a lemon. Later, she discovered the missing lemon on another table, but by then she was missing two pears. Finally, at her wits end and after she had given up the search for the fruit, the pieces mysteriously reappeared in almost exactly the same place where she had lost them.

"I guess George is up to his old tricks again," she told the staff later.

The 1848 House is open for Sunday Brunch and for private parties. For reservations call: (404) 428-1848.

THE KENNESAW HOUSE

THE KENNESAW HOUSE
MARIETTA, GEORGIA

Some speculate that The Kennesaw House, one of the oldest buildings in Marietta, Georgia, is home to over 700 ghosts. We know that thousands of people seeking comfort and shelter have crossed its threshold for the past 130 years just as they still do today. The three-story brick building, originally erected as an inn for the train depot passengers across the street, has served also as a Confederate and Union hospital, a Union morgue, a boarding house, and now the Marietta Museum of History inhabits the second floor, and The Kennesaw House, a fine restaurant, occupies the first floor.

When the author stood on the opposite side of the railroad tracks to take the building's picture, she sensed the presence of many forces. She couldn't identify any specific one, but she felt as if many people had traveled past that spot and maybe even died there. Her intuitions were not deceptive.

In 1853 Dix Fletcher built a "breakfast house" to serve the occupants of the passenger trains who unloaded on the opposite corner and called his establishment the "Fletcher House."

In 1862 Mary Starr and Col. V.M. White leased the thirty-two-room hotel from Dix Fletcher and changed the name from the Fletcher House to The Kennesaw House, the name it is called today. (1)

On April 12, 1862, the James J. Andrews Raiders, Yankee spies who invaded Marietta and stole a locomotive beginning "The Great Locomotive Chase," spent the night in hotels in

Marietta, Georgia. The Yankee infiltrators entered the Confederate State of Georgia under disguise and stole one locomotive, "The General," and three box cars from the train depot in Kennesaw, then named Big Shanty, and headed north towards Chattanooga. In an effort to prevent the communication of their actions, the raiders tried to damage the rails behind them and cut the telegraph lines. Fortunately, the Yankees were spotted leaving the station, and a great pursuit sprang forth by the fearless Conductor William A. Fuller and Engineers Jeff Cain and Anthony Murphy. These three men raced on foot the distance of two miles in chase of "The General" and began "The Great Locomotive Chase." They hopped onto an abandoned platform car and propelled it until they reached the Etowah River, where they switched the car for a locomotive. Fuller, Cain and Murphy raced in hot pursuit of the Raiders until they reached the approach to Kingston Station, where the Confederates had to abandon their engine because of south-bound trains. They pursued the outlaws again on foot until they reached Rome, Georgia. The engineers were in luck, however, because "The General" also had been forced to wait for south-bound trains. In Rome the Confederates jumped onto another locomotive, "The William R. Smith," which was under full steam and ready to roll and continued their pursuit.

The engineer on a Confederate train heading south, "The Texas," spotted "The General" and recognized the Yankee Raiders as spies. "The Texas" turned around and raced after "The General," catching up with it at Ringgold. When "The Texas" closed in behind, the Raiders abandoned their "General" and jumped. James J. Andrews had ordered his Raiders to escape in any way possible. Fortunately, all the Raiders were soon captured and imprisoned at Swims Jail in Chattanooga. Eight, including Andrews, were eventually hanged. Eight escaped from the prison to rejoin their Union forces, and six others were eventually freed;

the Yankees exchanged their Confederate prisoners of war for the remaining Raiders. The great adventure gained a tremendous amount of notoriety on both sides and became know as "The Great Locomotive Chase," and the Yankee Raiders received the Medal of Honor for their valor. (2)

William Pittenger's book, *The Great Locomotive Chase*, includes the tale of one of the Raiders who escaped and survived to tell his story:

> "In the Tremont House, the greater part of us registered names—either our own or others—and were soon sleeping soundly—the last time we slept in bed for many weary months!
>
> "Andrews was with the larger party in the hotel near the railroad station [Fletcher House], while four others, among whom were our three engineers, were in the other hotel at some distance. Two of these were not awakened in time for the next morning's train, and the other two were barely able to get over. Had they been a few moments later, the great railroad adventure, with all its excitement and tragedy, would not have been." (2)

Some of the Raiders stayed at the Marietta Hotel, which was owned by Dix Fletcher's son-in-law, Henry Greene Cole. His middle daughter, Eliza Fletcher Emmons, had attended Antioch College with Mr. Ross, one of the Raiders. At the time of the raid, she wasn't in town. Had she been, she would have recognized Mr. Ross as a Yankee, informed authorities, and the plot to steal the locomotive could have been foiled. After the Raiders had been captured by the Confederates, Mr. Ross wrote to Miss Fletcher, hoping to get her to intercede for him and save his life. But she did not respond to his pleas, and Mr. Ross was hanged along with the other Raiders. (2)

In August 1863 the hotel was taken over by the Confederate Army as a hospital for the sick and wounded. Ella Newsom, an experienced nurse from Tennessee, was ordered by Dr. Samuel H. Stout, of The Army of Tennessee, to organize and set up hospital facilities in all the buildings surrounding the Public Square in Marietta, including The Kennesaw House.

The wounded arrived by box cars from the battlegrounds in the North and were unloaded as quickly as possible and taken into the buildings. But when the homes, public buildings and schools were all filled, the injured men were unloaded onto the grass, the roads, the walkways, and everywhere there was a vacant spot. According to many reports, there were too many soldiers to count, many dying before they could be helped. All the women of the town turned out to give aid in every way possible. Ella Newsom remained in charge in Marietta for a year. In July of 1864 the Yankees invaded Marietta and took over the facilities. Ella Newsom and the Confederate Army moved her hospital south to Atlanta. When the Confederates lost the battle of Atlanta, she was forced to move farther south to Forsyth, Macon and finally Albany. (3)

After the war, Ella Newsom was recognized for her hospital work and honored with the title of "Florence Nightingale of the Southern Army."

The Federals used the third floor of The Kennesaw House as a hospital and the fourth floor as a morgue. When Sherman and his troops moved out of Marietta, they bombed the hotel, but, fortunately, only the fourth floor was destroyed. Later the building was repaired and remained as it appears today. (4)

Intriguing tales of war and espionage are not all that have been left behind at The Kennesaw House. Strange supernatural phenomena occur which startle its inhabitants only momentarily, because the building carries with it so much history and mystique.

The Doctor

Dan Cox, the curator of the Marietta Museum of History, was standing in front of the elevator on the second floor talking to his wife one afternoon in 1994. An eery quiet suddenly surrounded them, and he realized that someone else was standing beside the elevator. It was a gentleman whom he had never seen before, about 5'7" in height, wearing a flat hat and a cream colored linen long-coat about mid thigh in length. The man also wore leather boots that reached his mid calf. Mr. Cox wondered if the man had been a doctor because the spirit gave him the impression that he demanded respect. After a few seconds the man disappeared. Mr. Cox said there had been a Dr. Wilder, from time to time, who treated guests residing at the Kennesaw House. After Dan witnessed the apparition, he was reminded again that the House had also been used as a hospital during the War Between the States.

Mr. Cox also reported that two other people have witnessed the man's appearance. He also confessed that from time to time the elevator comes up by itself to the second floor and the door opens, but no one is ever there.

Tap, Tap, Tap, on the Stairs

On another occasion when Mr. Cox was on his way down the back stairs, he heard the sound of tap, tap, tap, on the iron railing. The sound reminded him of a wedding ring hitting the iron bar. It moved down several steps and stopped, and then a few seconds later it continued its descent down the stairs, only stopping several times before disappearing completely.

An Operation

After first entering the museum on the second floor and before speaking to the curator Dan Cox, the author was overcome by a faint vision in the back of the huge hall. For only seconds she saw a primitive operation scene appear in the room. The gray silhouette of a tall, brawny man wearing suspenders with his shirt sleeves rolled up to his elbows and bending over a patient lying on a table became clearer with each passing second. The man was assisted by several attendants who were all working frantically, trying to do something to the patient that she couldn't make out. Perhaps it was amputate a limb, dress a chest wound, or remove shrapnel; she strained to find out, but the scene disappeared too fast. A grim-faced, short girl, with her hair pulled back in a bun and wearing a cap, stood at the foot of the table holding a candle for light in the dingy room. The feeling the author immediately absorbed from the scene was that of anguish, futility, and intense fear. Then as mysteriously and as soundlessly as the vision appeared, it faded away. She ran to the spot to see if she could visualize it better or somehow recapture it, but there was nothing like it in that area of the museum with its silent manikins displaying their beautiful 1860s ball gowns, military uniforms and other memorabilia.

The author didn't even know if the large room had been partitioned into smaller rooms at the time. It seemed as if it hadn't. She wondered if the vision had been her imagination playing tricks on her or if it had really appeared for her to see.

GHOSTS INHABIT A BUILDING
ON MARIETTA'S PUBLIC SQUARE
MARIETTA, GEORGIA

One of the buildings on the Public Square dates back to the 1860s and is still there today housing a shop. Its painted stamped tin ceiling is reminiscent of the late Victorian era, when that style became popular. In some areas of the shop, the bare brick walls have been exposed, lending a primitive atmosphere to the shop.

The owner, wanting to remain nameless, confided the following story. A woman died in a dentist's chair some years back, and her spirit still inhabits the store. Most of the activity that the owner notices occurs down in the basement. From time to time, he hears muffled voices, but he can never make out what is being said. Other times out of the corner of his eye, he sees shadows moving slowly along the walls. He claims to feel a presence from time to time, but he isn't scared because nothing else has happened to frighten him. The voices remain just whispers barely audible. These strange phenomena have occurred so many times that now he almost expects something unusual to happen when he enters the basement.

The owner claimed that in July 1995, when he renovated the store, the strange activity increased.

When I mentioned that through my research I discovered that the building had been used as a hospital during the War Between the States in the 1860s, he was very surprised. I suggested that the ghost activity might have originated with some of those deaths. He said that he would keep that information in mind the next time something happened.

Marietta Journal
November 8, 1888

THE STORY OF THE BRUMBY ROCKER
MARIETTA, GEORGIA

On the east side of Marietta, Georgia, lives a Mr. W. M.
Taylor, a carpenter. For several weeks his little daughter, some
six years old, was at the point of death. Fever had wasted her
little form, and one cheek had rotted away from infection. She
was a sad sight to look upon. A number of neighbors visited the
distressed family frequently and rendered any assistance in their
power.

Last Sunday night two weeks ago, a few neighbors called,
as the child in its emaciated and weakened state appeared as if
she would not live long. A gentleman present was beseeched to
offer prayer for the sick child. The little group knelt humbly, and
a fervent and earnest prayer was offered up to the sympathizing
Savior for the restoration to health of the little sufferer. After the
prayer, to the surprise of all, the little girl, in a weak but audible
voice, said she wanted to get into the rocking chair. This request
was granted, and she was tenderly lifted from the bed and placed
in the chair, her little form being snugly wrapped in a quilt.

Parties present tell us that the little girl then feebly said, "I
want someone to rock me." Her sister started to perform this
kindness, but before she reached or took hold of the chair, to her
astonishment and the astonishment of all present, the large
Brumby rocking chair commenced rocking gently to and fro,

without the aid of any person in the room. A person present said, "An angel seemed to have heard the plaintive cry of the little sufferer and with invisible hands rocked the child to sleep." No one moved. Each intently watched the chair as it voluntarily rocked.

Finally a few other neighbors were sent for, to witness the mysterious movement of the chair. No one could account for the singular motion. A gentleman caught hold of the chair, and it slid some twelve inches and then resumed its swaying motion. After a while the little patient dropped off into a soothing sleep, and the chair ceased rocking. When the child awoke from her slumbers and opened her eyes, the chair began rocking again, which was kept up all night.

We are informed that from that night, the child began to grow better and is now walking about the house, although a sad looking object with one of her cheeks partially wasted away.

Several have attempted to solve the puzzle, but the unseen force that rocked the chair remains a mystery.

Reliable parties who witnessed the affair verify this statement.

GENERAL WILLIAM T. SHERMAN'S ARMY
KENNESAW, GEORGIA

On North Main Street in Kennesaw, Georgia, a two-hundred-year-old frame house still resounds with echoes from a fractured energy field and perhaps even a time warp. This is a house where voices from ancient tragedies emerge out of nowhere and leave the current inhabitants shaken and even changed forever.

On sweltering summer evenings when the traffic has cleared and the residents have decided to sit awhile on their massive wraparound front porch, they are not disappointed. Before long the silence becomes heavy, a moment without the shrill sound of crickets or the constant buzz of the June bugs, and then it happens. Invisible horses' hooves clatter on the asphalt, sounding too faint at first to the human ear, but the dog begins barking, so the observers know it's happening. Then garbled voices resound in the distance amid the whinnying of hundreds of horses. A deep roar of noise emerges—marching feet, identified as an army approaching, Sherman's army.

Someone from the company yells, "Halt!"

Without warning, all movement ceases, and the deep stillness returns as if every horse and rider is waiting for a command.

A youthful voice rings out from the flank, "General Sherman! You can see Atlanta from the mountain!"

Hoofbeats scurry away amid cries from the crowd and die in the distance, heading in the direction of the rising ground.

A small boy calls out to the army from the porch, "Is that

you Sherman? Is that really you?"

The observers wait for the sound of a single horse to approach. It stops close by and then turns slowly away, heading toward Atlanta. The hoofbeats of the lone lead horse are soon followed by the footsteps of marching soldiers and the grinding of cannon wheels.

The seconds that pass seem like hours until the sounds fade into the distance, and the observers know that they have witnessed the marching army of General Sherman. After Sherman has gone, an aura permeates the stillness that no one can describe. Cold air seeps out from under the porches, and a mist of fog hovers where the army disappeared.

THE PUBLIC HOUSE RESTAURANT
ROSWELL SQUARE
ROSWELL, GEORGIA

The quaint 1854 brick building located on Roswell Square in Roswell, Georgia, was originally the third and final structure built for the Roswell Mill and used as its commissary. The building is now home to the Public House Restaurant and several ghosts who have made their presence known for the past fifty-plus years.

The mill, located directly behind the commissary, manufactured thread, cotton and woolen goods. The Roswell Manufacturing Company is said to have monopolized the trade in all general supplies for that area. The store, originally built for the mill workers, sold every product necessary for domestic and business life.

During the War Between the States, times grew very difficult. Clothes and food were in very short supply because most of the manufactured goods had been purchased by the Confederate Army. When the Confederate currency became useless, most of the store's supplies were obtained by bartering with real goods—chickens, eggs, meat, produce, chopped wood, etc.—that the store could turn around and sell again to someone else. Desperate families gathered early in the morning at the mill store in hopes of purchasing some of the small amounts of thread the company would sell for cash. Long lines formed, creating a mass of angry people outside the doors of the Public House when supplies ran out.

THE PUBLIC HOUSE RESTAURANT

During General Sherman's invasion, the building was used as a hospital, initially for the retreating Confederacy and later for the advancing Federal army. The staff of the Public House Restaurant claim that they have two resident ghosts. One, a seventeen-year-old Union Soldier, they call Michael. The staff speculate that he died in the building when it was used as a hospital. The other is a spirit of a lovely young girl they named Katherine.

Some of the staff think that the two spirits dine at the restaurant after hours because on several occasions one waitress has inspected the tables in the morning before the doors are opened, only to discover that one table in the corner has been disturbed. The napkins have been opened, silverware moved and wine glasses moved to a different spot, just as if someone had been eating there. The waitress swore that she left the table setting in perfect order the night before. Perhaps the two sit by candle light, listen to their ethereal music and reminisce about their past life.

THE GHOST OF THE PUBLIC HOUSE

KATHERINE

Three visitors have seen the apparition of a young girl whom they call Katherine and think she is Michael's young love. Other waiters and waitresses have sensed her presence at the top of the stairs, and one visitor actually believes that he saw her ghostly form standing there for a few seconds before it vanished. Although no one knows for sure who Katherine is, some speculate that she might have been a nurse who fell in love with the Yankee soldier and mysteriously met her death there in the building.

THE SPIRITS IN THE LOFT

The loft area, which was once used as a funeral home, is now a piano bar. Coffins were lowered down to the main floor through the large opening between the loft and the opposite wall. The loft area seemed to be an appropriate and peaceful home for Michael and Katherine for many years.

This area at the top of the steps to the loft is the location where the ghost activity occurs most. When the author entered the restaurant, she noticed creaking and groaning and loud crackling noise coming from the beams at the top of the steps. The waiter claimed that the strange clamor was caused by the motion of the people moving across the floor in the loft. At the time most of the people were just sitting quietly at their tables and were not scraping their chairs. But later that same afternoon, the area remained silent even though several people walked up and down the steps.

The manager of the restaurant has witnessed several phenomena. In 1995 on countless mornings when he first arrived in the restaurant, he noticed that the two-wing back chairs in the second floor loft were facing the window as if the two seated there had been looking out the window all night onto the square. Each night in preparation for work the following day, the staff customarily arranges the chairs so they are facing the room. Other members of the staff have also witnessed these chairs moved out of place and can't give an explanation for it. This phenomena has happened so many times that most of the employees confirm the strange activity. At first they thought these occurrences were spooky, but now they speculate that Michael and Katherine rest there often. The members of the staff have come to accept the moving chairs as part of the building. In fact, they even make a game of seeing how many times the chairs are turned back to face the window.

Dunwoody Shoe Shop

The smaller area of the restaurant built around 1920 and now partitioned by brick columns was originally the Dunwoody Shoe Shop. The manager of the restaurant has experienced some very strange incidents there, too. One afternoon between 12:00 and 1:00 p.m., the window shades shot up, beginning with the first one, and then the next, and the next, until all the windows were completely exposed to the hot afternoon sun—as if someone had walked along the front of the restaurant and activated each shade, causing it to retract. The manager said that had he not witnessed the change himself, he would not have believed it. Sometimes when he arrives at work in the morning, all the shades are up. He claimed that the shades had been completely drawn down the night before.

When any supernatural event occurs at the restaurant, the staff is still amazed, and they are reminded again and again, first hand, that death is not the end.

The Public House Restaurant specializes in fine dining and is open Monday-Thursday 11:30 a.m.-2:30 p.m. and 5:30-10:00 p.m. and Friday and Saturday 5:30-11:00 pm. (770) 992-1400.

THE MYSTERIOUS CLOSET
LAWRENCEVILLE, GEORGIA

A family living in Lawrenceville, Georgia, in the late 1980s concluded that their home must have been built over an ancient cemetery for black residents. When their daughter was seven years old, she saw the figure of a black man standing in her closet and digging with a shovel into the ground. He appeared again and again to her. Several people witnessed the apparition, but didn't know what to make of it.

Several years later the same young girl saw a black woman standing in her closet, holding a baby in her arms. Tears were streaming down the woman's cheeks, and she was sobbing hysterically. Then a few months later the young girl saw both the apparitions standing together and finally the scene made sense. The man, who wore black pants with long suspenders over a white shirt, was digging in the back of her closet. The woman, probably his wife, wearing a long brown dress, hovered beside him and wept uncontrollably as she glanced down at the lifeless baby in her arms.

The man must have been digging a grave for the infant child, but the owners of the home were never able to uncover any records of a cemetery located in that spot. As long as they lived there, the apparition appeared occasionally to their daughter and others, playing out a scene that could have happened over a hundred years before.

THE VICTORIAN MIRROR
LAWRENCEVILLE, GEORGIA

The Bagwells didn't know the origin of their Victorian mirror, only that it had been in the Bagwell family ever since the War Between the States. It had always hung over their marble-topped mahogany washstand, and even though it didn't match the washstand, it seemed to belong there. The glass of the mirror was filled with imperfections; ripples and bubbles marred the surface but never interfered with the fine, clear reflection.

One afternoon in the '80s, while their ten-year-old daughter was gazing into the mirror, she saw the image of an old woman staring back at her. The stern-looking woman appeared to be in her seventies and wore her hair pulled back into a tight bun.

Immediately, their daughter ran and told them of the image. At first they didn't believe her and thought her imagination had played tricks on her. Finally, they agreed to see for themselves. Right before their eyes was the image of a face peering out of the mirror just as their daughter had said. The woman seemed to be concentrating hard on something, almost as if she were examining herself in the mirror. After a few seconds the old woman's face vanished.

Several days later the woman's face appeared again, and over the years she appeared many times to the family. While searching through some old photographs, they found a picture of a stern old woman who resembled the face staring out of the mirror. Mr. Bagwell discovered that the picture was of his great Aunt Minnie, who died in her eighties an old maid.

Many people witnessed the appearance of great Aunt Minnie's face in the mirror. Once when the Bagwells were entertaining a Girl Scout troop for a sleep-over, six or seven of the girls saw Aunt Minnie. The other girls couldn't see her and wondered if it was just a joke being played on them.

The Bagwells moved three times over a period of twenty years, and the spirit moved with them each time, settling in and appearing mostly in their Lawrenceville, Georgia, home, but when the Bagwells moved to their retirement home on Jekyll Island, the spirit vanished. They decided that she preferred their Lawrenceville home over the new, smaller one.

THE TUCKER-NEWSOM PLACE
1859
MADISON, GEORGIA

The big white frame house sits back off the road a good ways and is now deserted, but it still gives the impression that it was once a grand home. Two towering chimneys and a broken windmill add to that fantasy, and fenced off by itself in the far corner of the front yard next to the Milledgeville Road, a small cemetery is surrounded by an elaborately scrolled antique wrought iron fence with the words Tucker-Newsom 1859 written into the design of the gate. A marble column monument over six feet tall stands in the center of the small fenced area and carries the names and dates of the former residents.

In 1805 property in Morgan county became available to settlers through a device known as the land lottery. In 1809 Whitfield Tucker was originally granted two hundred fifty acres as part of the lottery. On December 25, 1817, Whitfield Tucker bought two-hundred-fifty more acres which he gave this to his wife Elizabeth for a Christmas present. According to the records, he owned four slaves and farmed the property. In 1837 his daughter Edy Tucker married William Newsom and lived either on or near the farm. Beginning in 1853 Augustus Tucker paid rent for the land until he died in 1857. After that all the information about the Tucker family ends with the names of Tucker and Newsom 1859 written on the cemetery gate.

A previous owner thinks the house was built around the early

1900s by a Methodist minister for his family. Evidently the house owned by the Tuckers burned or somehow vanished because he doesn't ever remember finding foundations or ruins. He remembers the windmill standing beside the driveway ever since the 1940s and recalls that it was used to pump water up from the well for the dairy farm.

THE WHITE FORM OF A YOUNG GIRL

The house and farm land has changed hands many times over the years, and more recently the house was converted into a fine restaurant. There have been many reports of ghost sightings, and the most recent was by the waitresses who worked in the Hugs Restaurant. One afternoon one waitress went into the back hall and was startled by the appearance of a white figure of a girl standing by the stairs. The apparition stood there only for a minute before disappearing. On another night she saw the same figure float down the hall and disappear through the wall. At another time a different waitress heard footsteps in the hall late at night when no one else was there. Both girls attributed the phenomena to a legend that a young girl had hung herself in the upstairs hall; some said she was mourning the loss of a lover.

A GIRL CRYING

In the 1950s a woman worked as a maid for a family who lived in the house, and she claimed that the house was haunted, too. Often when she was coming to work in the morning, she heard the sounds of a girl crying, but never could make out where the noise was coming from. At other times she claimed to hear footsteps walking up and down the stairs. Other people confirmed that they had heard the footsteps, too.

The Large Dog

The children who walked along the road claimed that if they stepped off the road onto the grass for a second, a large dog appeared in the ditch and barked at them until they returned to the road. Some think the dog was real; others think the dog was a ghost. Some think that the dog was protecting the cemetery in the corner of the lot from intruders.

The Strange Girl

The most peculiar of all the stories is the one told by a former resident. Sometime in 1971 or 1972 a young girl he estimated to be in her early thirties came to the door and asked if she could talk to someone from the house. She confessed that she had been drawn to the house by some strange force and didn't understand why. At first she felt as if she had lived in the house at some time in another life. She claimed that she would go into a trance and see herself in the house living there, but something had prevented her from finishing the trance because she always came out of it before something terrible happened. But just recently, she had allowed herself to finish the trance. She said she saw herself in another lifetime in the house, and a party was going on downstairs. She remembers that she was so tired and so depressed that she went out onto the porch and hung herself from the railing. The young girl described the porch on the back of the house that the owner had recently enclosed. The back of the house was designed in such a way that it would have been impossible to see from the outside that there had ever been a porch there.

The young girl said that her name had been Beth or Elizabeth and that she was sure that she had been buried on the farm. The owner told her about the cemetery, and they went out to look.

THE TUCKER-NEWSOM PLACE

Sure enough they found a tombstone with the name of Beth written plainly on the front of the stone. When the girl saw this, she turned as white as the marble on the monument. She said that she had been about twenty-six or -seven years old when the tragedy happened. The owner never saw her again; but he said that as strange as the story sounds, he believed she was telling the truth. When they walked through the house, she told him things about the house that he had never heard before. She seemed to know how and where the house had been changed over the years, closets added and hallways cut from room to room. She claimed that the only way she knew any of these changes was because she had lived here in her other life.

Sarah's Wings

SARAH'S WINGS
MILLEDGEVILLE, GEORGIA

Bebe Jones had been visiting a friend who was a patient in the Oconee Regional Medical Center until late on that Thursday night in April of 1996. As a registered nurse she tried to help her friends through their difficult medical emergency. She was like that, always helping out anyone with a need. When she got into her automobile, she felt a little tired and dizzy, but she didn't worry because the drive home wasn't far. Her diabetes had been acting up lately, and she reminded herself to get this checked out. On the winding road near her home, she blacked out and lost control of her car, sending it crashing down a steep embankment. When the rescue workers carried her back to the hospital, there was barely a thread of life left in her body, and she soon died from massive injuries and a diabetic coma.

Her husband, Tom; her seven-year-old twins, Sarah and Stephen; and her nine-year-old son, Thomas, deeply mourned her death. The two boys couldn't bear to go to the funeral home because of how their mother looked after the accident. They didn't want to remember her that way.

When tragedy touches our families, God is still there watching over us and sends people to help give us comfort. A very cruel and difficult task for Sarah was to see her mother lying dead in the casket. This was a time she will probably never forget. But she insisted that she wanted to go. While she stood silently at her mother's side, a beautiful flower arrangement of sun flowers, sitting near the casket, caught her eye.

"These are my mommy's favorites," she said to her Dad and pulled two out. She carefully placed one in her mother's hand and kept one for herself, holding it tightly to her chest.

Worried about how she was taking this, her father ushered her out to another room so that they could be alone. A friend followed them and offered to take their picture. No one was prepared for what followed. Tom sat in a comfortable chair with Sarah, still clinging to the sun flower, nestled in his lap. While they waited for the Polaroid™ to develop, they were surprised at the strange shape that began to appear on the film. Huge angel wings materialized in the photo behind the two sitting in the chair. No one knew if the film was defective or if the image was formed by the shadow of the lamp.

But immediately, Sarah said, "That's my mommy watching over us." Her father's friend tried to take several more pictures, but not one turned out.

In the face of this terrible tragedy, the Lord sent his comforter to give hope that death is not the end, and that life is eternal. This picture has inspired the entire Jones family, and now it is used to inspire others. It gives us evidence that God is there on the other side, watching, waiting, and helping by sending his angels to lift us up out of our despair.

THE HOMESTEAD
MILLEDGEVILLE, GEORGIA

One of the oldest houses in Milledgeville, The Homestead, built around 1818, stands today as a true memorial to the antebellum years. Five generations of the Williams family have owned the house and preserved a life-style all but forgotten to most. For The Homestead, the South is not dead, but very much alive. The Homestead's beautiful English boxwood gardens, which were planted in the 1820s by the first owner, Lucinda Parke, are nostalgic reminders of the past and mingle their faint aroma with the sweet wisteria, heady magnolia, antique camellias and wandering jasmine during the flowering season of each one to form a potpourri of scents found only in the deep south.

Ghosts live at The Homestead, too, and make their presence known regularly. On one hot summer evening in 1986, when Fielding D. Whipple, Deacon of the Baptist church next door, was leaving a meeting and going to his car, he heard a voice call, "Please, Oh. . . . Please don't leave me. I'm hearing noises in my house."

It was the late Katherine Scott sitting on the back steps of The Homestead. She had been living in The Homestead with Fanny Way Ferguson for several years and knew almost every one in town. She was also a great story teller and loved ghost tales, so little thumps and bumps didn't ordinarily frighten her.

"I've called the police. I don't want to stay here by myself until I can get the house checked. I think someone may be in there. I've heard footsteps all evening, and I know no one is upstairs tonight.

Mr. Whipple agreed to walk with her through the house. They walked from room to room and all seemed quiet. It was a very hot summer night in July and all the windows in the house had been opened. The air was as still as a tomb and heavy with humidity. All the doors in the house were also propped open, but when they reached the third floor, the door to the general's room was shut.

During the War Between the States, a general from the Confederate Army was hidden away in an attic room in The Homestead for several months because he suffered from pneumonia. He was too sick to travel with his troops when they abandoned the city, and he was hiding in The Homestead when Sherman and his army occupied Milledgeville. But, unfortunately, he died shortly afterwards. Ever since, the family swore his ghost remained as an unsettled spirit in that room because many times they found a mysterious depression in the pillow on his bed and the covers disheveled. Other times the family complained of hearing footsteps. So ever since the general died, the room was referred to as the general's room.

Mr. Whipple and Ms. Scott opened the door to the general's room, but found nothing out of the ordinary. They returned down the stairs, but on the way they were frightened to death by the tremendous slam of the general's door. They did not want to return to the room, but they forced themselves to go back and open the door. Satisfied that everything was in good order, the two headed back down the stairs. When they reached the first floor, the silence was broken again by the thunderous slam of the general's door.

By then the police had arrived, and they, too, walked through the house to check for prowlers. After checking under all the beds and closets, they opened the door to the general's room, but found all in good order. After propping the door open, they returned downstairs. But just as they agreed that all was well, the thunderous slam from the general's door reverberated through the house.

The big policeman looked around and then finally said, "Well if the general wants the door to his room closed, then leave it closed."

Perhaps the spirit was still afraid he'd be discovered after all these years.

LOCKERLY HALL

THE GHOSTS OF LOCKERLY HALL
MILLEDGEVILLE, GEORGIA

In 1852 the wealthy land owner and planter Daniel Reese Tucker built a lovely plantation home for his wife, Martha Goode of Virginia, and his five children and named it Rose Hill. Since their first home in Milledgeville was destroyed by a tornado and the second house was ravaged by fire, he vowed that this planter's mansion would be an edifice that "neither fire nor wind could destroy." And it is. The beautiful Georgian mansion has weathered the decay of age, the ravages of war and the 1880s earthquake, an act of God so powerful that it destroyed part of Charleston and left a small crack in the foundation of Rose Hill.

When Milledgeville was still the capitol of Georgia, Rose Hill glittered in a social whirl of parties and gained the reputation of hosting the grandest and most prestigious receptions and balls in the state. Satins upholstered the delicate French furniture popular during the French Napoleonic era, and the interior sparkled with many fine pieces of Chinese export porcelain, Limoges china and priceless Venetian Crystal chandeliers. Visitors claimed the entrance resembled a Greek temple. The main hall was floored with 12" squares of black and white Italian marble, and the woodwork was embellished with a faux marble design still evident today.

Mr. Tucker was one of the largest slave owners in the South, counting approximately 800 at one time as members of his plantation. His land holdings included thousands of acres in Baldwin and Bibb Counties and stretched west to Hawkinsville, a 45-minute drive by car, and almost reaching Sandersville to the south. Family members have said that a man could ride all day on horseback in any direction and never reach the end of his property. Included in this tract were holdings that became the largest and purest deposits of white gold—Kaolin—in the world. Kaolin is a clay used in the process of making fine china. Georgians didn't know the value of the white clay until the 1930s when the rich Georgia deposits were discovered. In the 1860s this land was considered poor for growing crops and of little value. After the War Between the States, land was confiscated from the plantation owners and generously given away to the newly freed slaves. That is one of the reasons why a large majority of the people living in these counties are black. Their ancestors were the slaves who worked on these plantations.

In the 1920s the home passed out of the family and was bought by R. W. Hatcher, who renamed it Lockerly Hall after his ancestral home in Scotland, and it has been called that ever since. Both he and his lovely wife lived out their days happily at Lockerley and died there.

Today the mansion is used as the guest house for ECC International Inc., a company devoted to exporting Kaolin all over the world. Many of the business executives visiting Lockerley Hall have referred to it as the ghost house.

Emma Tucker The Ghost

Several family members died in the house, including the original owners Daniel and Martha Tucker, their daughter Emma Tucker and her husband, George Sibley, but no one knows for sure the identity of the lovely ghost of a young woman. Visitors to Lockerley call her Emma and speculate that she is Emma Tucker, who married George Sibley, son of the wealthy Josiah

Sibley from Augusta, on January 21, 1862. George later prospered by owning many textile mills around the South. Some think that Emma lived out her years in heartache and discontent, forced to marry a man she didn't love. Yet, others say that the two were very happy and lived a long and prosperous life together.

When carpenters and painters began work on the restorations in the early 1950s, they were surprised to witness the apparition of a young woman dressed in a long, flowing white gown appear in the front left bedroom on the second floor. She stood there for only a few seconds and smiled at them as if to give her approval of their changes. Then she vanished. When the men related the story to the others, they swore that not one of them had been drinking and that each one saw the same vision simultaneously. After that episode the painters were leery about entering that room for any reason. Over the years the spirit acquired the name Emma, a name she is called today. But no one is sure of the true identity of the spirit.

PEELING PAINT

According to one of the carpenters, John Adcock, another mystery occurred in that same bedroom. Only days after the first sighting of the beautiful lady, all the paint in the bedroom now referred to as Emma's room began to peel off the wall in little pieces. The painters were overcome by the mystery and didn't know what had caused the dilemma that materialized overnight. At first they blamed the type of paint, but this was the same type used all over the house. The painters were ultimately forced to scrape every piece of paint off the wall before repainting it with the same color. This episode of peeling paint never occurred again in any other room.

THE FRIGHTENED GUEST

In 1994 when the house was full of guests from England, an older gentleman slept in Emma's room. During the night, he awoke just in time to witness a lovely lady crawling into bed with him. Hysterical, he jumped out of bed and grabbed all his belongings, but before he could leave the room, she vanished. He ran half naked down the stairs, out the front door and vowed that he'd never return to Lockerley again.

After that episode, many men have asked to sleep in Emma's room, but no one has ever reported seeing her.

A STRANGE VOICE

In 1995 when another visitor spent the night in Emma's room, Emma seemed unusually distressed by the intrusion. The visitor began brushing her hair in front of the lovely Victorian marble topped dresser and mirror just as she did at home before going to bed. Without warning, she heard a soft voice behind her say, "You shouldn't be sleeping in my room." That and no more.

The experience upset the visitor dreadfully, so much so that she rushed across the hall to see if her room might be changed. The visitor was greatly relieved when her accommodations were moved to the room next door. When the woman returned to Emma's room to retrieve her clothes and toiletries, the apparition of a lady dressed in a long, flowing white nightgown stood in front of the fireplace. The hair on the visitor's arms shot up straight, and she was too frightened to enter the room. She begged the other guest to assist her in collecting her belongings. When they returned to the room, the figure had vanished.

The visitor immediately moved all her things to the next room and never returned.

THE OLD MAN

A closet once existed on the first floor near the breakfast room. This area is now a hall, and to the right of it is a stair for the servants to carry the laundry to the second floor. One dreary afternoon, an elderly man around eighty years old was seen standing there wearing a long trench coat. He just vanished and was never seen again.

Martha Tucker told her great granddaughter many stories about the people and incidents that happened at Lockerly. In the 1860s when her grandfather, Daniel R. Tucker, was wheelchair bound with arthritis, his servant pushed the wheelchair over a hole in the floor inside the pantry (a location near the stair) three times a day. This opening, which was once used as a silent butler, was positioned directly over the huge wood-fired cook stove. The elder Mr. Tucker received heat treatments from the steam rising up from the kettles on the wood stove below. Could it be possible that Mr. Tucker's spirit still roams lovely Lockerley Hall today?

THE BURGLAR ALARM

One Sunday morning the alarm went off. The guest house manager was informed, and she cautiously entered the home, not knowing what she would find. Her husband was with her, so she had decided not to call the police right away. The first floor seemed exactly as she had left it, nothing out of place. She slowly walked up the stairs, and when she reached the second floor, she immediately noticed that the door at the end of the hall was open.

Because all the windows to the mansion have been nailed shut and the doors are double locked, the manager wondered how the door to the balcony could have been left open. When she reached Emma's room, she saw that the covers had been turned down and the pillow was sitting at a strange angle in the middle of the bed as if someone had been adjusting it. The manager tried to justify everything that happened, but she often wonders if Emma had unwittingly opened the door to the balcony for some fresh air and returned to bed only to disappear when the burglar alarm went off.

The housekeeper swore that the bed had been completely made up and the doors locked before she left the night before. The manager has always checked the rooms before she leaves the house, just to make sure they will be ready if a guest arrives unannounced, and she remembers that all was well when she left the night before.

YANKEES AT LOCKERLY

A family member from Augusta revealed a story about her great-grandmother, Martha Tucker, standing at the front gate of Rose Hill when Sherman and his Yankee army marched by:

> "The soldiers didn't burn the house, but they looted and stole everything of value. They burned all the outbuildings, including the slave quarters and horse barns. They stole all the livestock and animals, leaving the family with nothing to eat."

Her great-grandfather was an invalid at the time and remained in the house during the siege. Mrs. Tucker thought Sherman decided not to burn the house because Mr. Tucker was so sick. Maybe after losing two homes earlier in his life, God spared him this final loss.

THE LAST SUPPER
MILLEDGEVILLE, GEORGIA

While visiting a local yard sale, a collector of religious pictures found a lovely etching depicting the famous scene of Christ at the Last Supper. The price seemed rather high, but she immediately felt drawn to the emotionally moving picture with its elaborate gilt frame. The collector anguished over the purchase, returning to the picture several times before offering to buy it at a lower price.

The owners confessed that their sale contained items which had belonged to their late mother, and this picture had been a favorite of hers. It had hung in her bedroom and given her strength during her long, painful illness with cancer. They decided not to keep the picture because it reminded them too much of their mother's suffering before she died. Still, it was too special for them to sell at a lower price.

After haggling back and forth, the collector finally bought the famous scene. From the first moment she placed the picture in her car, she experienced physical discomfort. By the time she reached home, she had a splitting headache. She tried to ignore it and placed *The Last Supper* in the room where she displayed all her other religious scenes. Some of her favorites were Jesus praying at Gethsemane, Mary leaving Jesus's crucifixion with John and Jesus entering Jerusalem surrounded by the people waving palms and children carrying flowers, depicting Palm Sunday. She was quite thrilled to have found *The Last Supper* and knew it would be a wonderful addition to her collection.

Weeks passed, and *The Last Supper* remained on the floor propped against the bookshelf. At one point the collector experienced so much discomfort upon looking at the picture that she turned the face back against the shelves. Not knowing what was causing her discomfort, she finally made up her mind to hang the picture once and for all. She selected a spot at the very top of one corner of the room, where the gold gilt from the frame would draw the eye upward. At first the picture was a handsome addition. But soon the comforting peace seemed to have disappeared from her favorite room. She rarely went in just to sit anymore. She would go in and pick up a book, look around at her once-inviting reading space and then leave, feeling a vague tension in the room.

One afternoon not long afterwards, her daughter visited the room to search for a favorite book.

"There is something fighting in this study," the daughter said. "It sounds strange to say this, but I can't help but feel the tension."

The collector knew immediately where that strange feeling was coming from—the picture of the Last Supper. There seemed to be a spirit attached to it that didn't want it in her collection. With regret, she immediately removed the lovely scene and took it to a Friday morning yard sale nearby. By the time she arrived across town, she had developed another headache, and when she gave the picture to the lady running the sale, her temples were pounding.

"Please, just sell this picture or give it away. I . . . ah . . . . can't use it," she said.

The woman was confused but took the picture saying, "It is so lovely. Maybe you could use the frame. I can't imagine why you want to sell it. I'll give you what I get for it."

"No. You can keep whatever you get. Just sell it. This picture has a strange spirit attached to it. I get a headache whenever I'm around it." Not wanting to explain anything else about the picture, the collector left. The collector was not surprised when her favorite room returned to its former peaceful retreat. The tension had mysteriously disappeared from her gallery of religious pictures.

The collector rarely thought of the etching except when she saw another rendition of the Last Supper; then she wondered what had become of it. In the spring of 1994, only a year after she'd given the Bible scene away, she held her own yard sale. During the course of the day, a sweet lady lingered and showed some interest in the antiques offered for sale. During the conversation, the lady introduced herself as Shirley and admitted that she collected religious pictures and other memorabilia. Then Shirley excitedly told the story of buying her prized possession, an etching of the Last Supper with a beautiful gilt frame. Shirley claimed that the proprietor of the yard sale confessed that a strange woman had just given it to her to sell out of the blue. Shirley hung it in her dining room and felt as if it were part of her family. She admitted that she had suffered with cancer for years and endured countless operations, showing the scars on her arms where she had received medication. But miraculously, this past year she had been completely well.

When Shirley described where she had found the scene, the collector knew the picture was the same one she'd given away to the yard sale the year before. The collector realized that the picture had never been meant for her, but for Shirley, who had suffered with cancer the way the previous owner had. The collector realized, too, that some things are just not meant to be, like her ownership of this picture.

THE OLD STATE PRISON FARM

THE OLD STATE PRISON FARM
MILLEDGEVILLE, GEORGIA

It seems as if the former prisoners from the Old State Prison built in 1911 in Milledgeville, Georgia, are reaching out for help. Larry Findley, an employee of the correctional institution of Georgia, has become very interested in preserving the prison for historical purposes, and his dream is to one day turn the building into a museum. The ominous brick structure, resembling a warehouse, was the site of the first electric chair execution in Georgia. Findley doesn't want the boarded up and disintegrating building to be torn down and is afraid that the owners, Forstmann & Co., will do just that.

Since 1994 Findley has worked diligently to research and record the names of the prisoners buried in the overgrown cemetery at the back of the five-acre prison yard. Many times family members search in vain for a father or mother. Now a complete listing will be available and will give the inmates some dignity at the end of their lives. For some reason Larry feels compelled to pursue his task, so much so, that he has let other responsibilities slide. He admits, too, that he doesn't understand why he can't do anything else. Perhaps the spirits are behind his motivations; perhaps they are leading him in his search.

When the author stood outside the six-foot anchor fencing to take a photograph of the old prison, the ancient pecan trees surrounding her clicked and cracked so loudly, in a perfectly calm day, that she was sure there were many spirits there. When she tried to push the lever on her camera to advance the film, the lever, surrounding disc and screw came apart in her hand. Something had inadvertently unscrewed the lever without her knowing it. A split second later, she returned to her car and left, afraid of what might happen next.

In the 1930s the cemetery was just an overgrown field, but after being left unattended for the past sixty years, it has now become a forest. Many of the license-plate type numbers identifying the graves have been stolen or simply rusted over the years and fallen off the concrete grave markers. Findley's job isn't an easy one, and not one without its own perils. The records are poorly written and scanty at best, so his research has led him into the Atlanta Archives searching out the prisoners' original death certificates.

It was on one of his visits to the forgotten graves, obscured by the overgrowth of trees and vines, that he first felt the gentle touch of a hand on his shoulder. The experience frightened him, but when he looked around, no one was there. Then he felt the gentle pressure on his back guiding him in the direction of a clearing nearby. Unable to see any identifying plates, he decided to take a picture. When the photo was developed, he was surprised to see the cloudy images of what he thinks are spirits, probably spirits of the dead prisoners. Whenever he is in this area, words come into his head: "Let me tell you my story," or "Let us tell our stories." The entire experience has shaken him, but he can't forget about these prisoners.

Another episode happened while Findley stood in the middle of a cleared area which to him resembled a grave. Years earlier a shovel had been thrown into the weeds beside the grave and still lay there rusting away. He felt something brush briskly against the back of his neck, and then some force pushed his hat forward so far that it covered his forehead. He was ready to take a picture and wound the film forward to the next frame when mysteriously the camera button clicked by itself. When the picture was developed, two red columns of light appeared to be coming up out of the bushes. He wonders whether the red column of light is evil or not. The idea worries him, but nothing else has happened there. Perhaps the spirits are trying to communicate with him to let him know that they are glad he is doing this work.

While investigating some of the inmates' records, Findley has discovered that the prisoners may have suffered inhumane treatment. Many of the death certificates indicate that the cause of the prisoner's death was cerebral hemorrhage or a fractured skull, suggesting that beatings were common. In the female prison located across the highway, women prisoners frequently had their babies buried with them. Many death certificates identified young infants who had died of pneumonia buried with their mothers. Findley uncovered records saying that a sixteen-year-old boy had been executed for horse stealing and for breaking and entering.

Larry Findley still feels a deep compassion for these lost inmates and is determined to complete the records and continue his crusade in creating a museum out of the Old State Prison Farm.

For more information contact:
The Georgia Prison Historical Society
P.O. Box 1356
Hardwick, Georgia 31034
(912) 452-1626

THE CEMETERY
MILLEDGEVILLE, GEORGIA

When the young man drove past the pillars of the cemetery gate, the car radio blared defiantly, instantly interrupting the peaceful setting usually generated by the giant oaks and cedars that had shaded the graves for almost a hundred years. On other days he often sat quietly under the trees in contemplation, enjoying the solitude. But on this day, he was singing at the top of his lungs to the tune, "Sweet Caroline," and thinking about the coming evening he would spend with his lovely new girlfriend. She was everything he'd ever dreamed of having in a partner, and he marveled that they seemed meant for each other from the beginning. How he ever found her, he'd never know. He imagined that they must be soul mates, although he didn't "believe in all that crap."

Out of the corner of his eye, he spotted a lovely bouquet of new silk lilacs arranged in a vase on one of the graves. Faded silk and plastic flowers marked grave sites everywhere he turned, left by some caring mourner to weather away and arranged haphazardly in the bronze vases to somehow enhance the otherwise indistinguished memorial plaques. Their presence gave the cemetery an artificial look that usually made him want to turn away. But this time the flowers drew him to the spot. They were just what he needed to surprise his girlfriend, and he was sure she'd love him forever for the gesture.

The grave was located directly across an isle only several feet away from a large marble statue of Jesus. The grass had

THE CEMETERY

been allowed to grow up around the statue's feet as well as the many nearby graves, giving that part of the cemetery a shabby look. But the lavender silk lilacs stood out high above all the other flowers, fresh and new, heralding a lovingly cared for grave.

When he swooped down and grabbed up the bouquet, he didn't notice that the ground had been recently disturbed. After several long strides he returned to his car, with its radio screaming out tunes; he was so happy that he didn't care who complained. He nervously glanced around for witnesses to his little crime, but the place was deserted.

"No one will ever miss them," he told himself, trying to push away pangs of guilt. "And when they do. . . . Ha! Ha! Ha! It will be too late. Dead people are dead, and they don't care one way or the other about flowers or anything else for that matter."

Just the same, he had never stolen anything in his life before and wondered what had provoked him to take these flowers. He threw them onto the cluttered back seat of his car and took off.

By the time he picked up his girlfriend that evening, he had forgotten all about the flowers. They still lay in a heap in the back seat with all his other junk: a football, his army camouflage jacket, some empty beer and coke cans he'd intended to recycle and some fishing equipment.

Weeks passed, and he had forgotten all about the flowers until one dreary day when he decided to clean out the back seat of his car. He picked up the lilacs one by one, straightened some, brushed off any dust and gathered them into a lovely arrangement, all the while contemplating giving the flowers to his girlfriend and imagining her reaction. It was their three month anniversary. He knew she would be excited. But the idea of remorse over stealing them from the cemetery never crossed his mind.

The young man leaped up the three steps to his porch and was greeted by an elderly man with long gray hair, whiskers and cold, beady eyes, sitting in the rocking chair. He'd never seen the man before and wondered what he wanted. An eerie stillness surrounded the young man now, and he shivered from some unexplainable chill in the eighty-five degree air.

The stranger pointed with a painfully thin white finger to the bouquet of lilacs and said in a horse, raspy voice, "What are you doing with my flowers? I don't take kindly to thievery, and I want you to put them back."

The young man didn't know what to say. How could this man know where these flowers came from? He didn't believe the strange man.

"I don't know what you are talking about, Mister. Where did you come from anyhow, and what are you doing sitting here on my porch?"

With fierce indignation, the old man stared the young man straight in the eye without flinching. "Those flowers came from my grave, and I want them back."

After that comment the old man mysteriously disappeared. The porch area was filled with a dank, musty odor resembling wet dirt. When the young man looked at the rocker, which was still rocking, he discovered fresh clay on the cement porch where only moments earlier the man's feet had rested.

Terrified, the young man jumped back into his car and raced immediately to the cemetery, afraid that he'd never be able to find the right grave. Sure enough the plaque where the flowers came from displayed the name of a recently deceased gentleman around the age of the old man who appeared on the porch. The bare earth over the grave had been disturbed recently. One stray piece of lilac lay across the bronze name plate, and the young man nervously arranged the flowers in the vase as neatly as he could.

He apologized profusely to the deserted grave site before quietly tiptoeing away. He never again returned to the spot.

The young man married the lovely girl, but to this day, he has never forgotten the incident or stolen anything again as long as he lived.

SISSY WILLIS IN HER WEDDING DRESS

SISSY WILLIS—THE GHOST OF THE WILLIS HOUSE
MILLEDGEVILLE, GEORGIA

The beloved Sissy Willis is still managing the affairs of the Willis House just as she did when she was alive, says the owner, Saralyn Latham, and she couldn't do without Sissy's help. Saralyn always loved the house she remembers visiting as a child because Sissy Willis was her grandmother's sister and her wonderful great aunt who loved to entertain and created an atmosphere of hospitality.

"She always had a houseful of people," said Saralyn. And Saralyn has carried on the tradition by using the house for a restaurant and catering service. But she never dreamed that Sissy's spirit would still be there. It was a wonderful surprise.

The Willis House was built between 1828 and 1832 by Moses Forte, a professor at Midway Seminary, a woman's seminary of Oglethorpe University in Milledgeville, Georgia. Nestled on a high hill amid towering magnolia trees, the Willis House is just across the street from the original site of the woman's seminary, now owned by the Baldwin County Board of Education. A school has remained on that same spot for over one hundred and sixty years. Saralyn Latham was thrilled when she stumbled onto a ledger that had been hidden in the back of the attic for years. It dates from 1834-1837 and is stamped by the original owner, Moses Forte, and helps in part to date the age of the house.

In 1898 the home was bought by Dawson Willis, who gave it to his beloved second wife, Estelle, as a wedding present in 1911. Estelle was better known as Sissy and lived in the fourteen-room house until her death at age 92. They never had any children together, but Sissy helped raise Dawson's two daughters from a previous marriage.

When Mrs. Latham first bought the house, she removed all the beautiful Oriental carpets and sent them to Atlanta to be cleaned. The entire house was turned topsy-turvy, scrubbed and redecorated in Mrs. Latham's taste because she intended to open a catering service for parties and weddings.

HAIR PINS

That first year after Mrs. Latham opened her business, her staff found large antique hair pins dropped on the carpets in various rooms at different times, mostly the dining room. Latham noticed that these were the same kind of old-fashioned hair pins that Sissy wore when her long hair was pulled up high into a French twist. They discovered the pins frequently during that first year, but in the years that followed the incidence of finding the pins decreased. Still, every once in a while, one of the members of Mrs. Latham's staff will find one just lying on top of the carpet.

OVER-COOKED VEGETABLES

Sissy Willis loved to entertain a crowd of friends, and over the years she gained a reputation for cooking wonderful meals. She strongly disliked over-cooked vegetables, however, and claimed that this was one way to ruin a meal.

When Saralyn is entertaining a large crowd and all pots are cooking on all the burners, the electricity suddenly cuts off under the pot where the vegetables are becoming over-cooked. This happens often and without fail. Sometimes even the oven turns off by itself.

SARALYN LATHAM WITH THE WEDDING MIRROR'S STRANGE IMAGE

Members of Mrs. Latham's staff are great believers in ghosts, and whenever the stove cuts off, every one remarks, "Sissy's here with us today."

THE WEDDING MIRROR

In 1988 the wedding reception of a senator's daughter was held at the Willis House. Many of the pictures taken of the couple were taken in the dining room in front of the beautiful gilt-framed mirror hanging over the huntboard. Not long after the wedding, Mrs. Latham received a call from the bride's mother saying they had captured an image of a ghost in the mirror in the dining room. It resembled the reflection of a lady in a long flowing gown. The shape of the figure imitated the form of Sissy Willis's wedding gown, which is pictured in a small photograph hanging in the hall. This strange form always appears when a photo is taken of the reflection of the mirror hanging over the buffet in the dinning room. Even when the photographer turned off the lights and moved to several different positions, the image was still there, although you couldn't see it with the naked eye. One of the men used a video camera without any flash or bright light, and the mysterious form appeared then, too.

The author used her own camera and stood in many different locations in the dining room taking the pictures. Whether the large chandelier was off or on, the ghostly form still appeared in the mirror on the photograph, only changing in size and shape.

Mrs. Latham thought that Sissy Willis's step-daughter had been married in the house, perhaps in Sissy's dress, but she could only speculate if Sissy had been married in the house.

The Bedroom Door

According to all reports, Sissy Willis chose the lovely room behind the formal dining room to be her bedroom and slept there for most of her life. Now, the bedroom is used as a bride's room when a wedding is held. When entertaining large groups for wedding receptions and anniversary parties, however, Mrs. Latham leaves the door to the bedroom closed. On numerous occasions, Mrs. Latham has returned in the morning only to find the door to the bedroom standing wide open, opening into the dining room. She is sure that she closed the doors the night before.

Perhaps Sissy's spirit leaves the bedroom in the early morning hours, opens the bedroom door and walks through the dining room, dropping her hair pins along the way. One thing is certain, though, Sissy's spirit is still busy in the Willis House.

THE NATIVITY SCENE
MILLEDGEVILLE, GEORGIA

When I found the beautiful nativity figurines at a local yard sale one Saturday in August, I hesitated buying the set because the statue of Mary was missing. Over and over again I returned to the table displaying the large, detailed porcelain figurines of Joseph, the three wise men, a donkey, a shepherd with sheep and the baby Jesus and wished that the mother Mary hadn't been lost. I finally gave in and bought the set, hoping that somewhere I might find the missing piece. The owner halfheartedly promised to look for Mary and insisted that he'd call me if he found her. Behind our pleasant smiles, we both knew that Mary had been lost long ago.

Unfortunately, my weakness of trying to save antiquated and broken relics from the trash heap has filled our basement and attic with long forgotten mementoes of just this type. I reminded myself of the lovely chair without a seat, broken pot, dresser without a foot, doll without hair and clothes and several empty frames, to name a few. But at that moment I promised myself I wouldn't forget about the manger scene. I wouldn't forget about Mary.

Every week I said a small prayer to myself when I ventured to another yard sale, "Please Lord, let me find a Mary for this nativity scene."

Doubts set in, and I told myself how dumb it was to expect God to act in the completion of my treasure hunt. But I placed the set of figurines behind glass on the shelf of my china closet in plain view to remind me of my mission. I was sure that God would assist me in the hunt.

September and October passed without success. I not only didn't find a replacement, but I didn't see another manger scene. November passed, too, and even the middle of December arrived without any success of my mission. I searched all the stores for a replacement, but most scenes sold with all the figurines in one set. In order to get the Mary figurine, I was forced to buy an entire nativity. I wasn't prepared to make such an extravagant expenditure right before Christmas.

On Christmas Eve when I passed the display of the manger scene resting on my living room coffee table, I felt a stab of remorse at the sight of the missing Mary. The figures appeared so lonely and forlorn, part of their meaning displaced. The idea of the Christ Child, of Jesus, growing up without a mother was too painful to imagine. What would have become of him, I pondered? For many of us the presence of the Holy Mother, Mary, carries tremendous significance. God's miracle of Mary, the virgin, giving birth is an integral part of the first Christmas story.

That night, as I served punch at the church Christmas party, I was haunted by the vision of Jesus growing up without a mother. As hard as I tried to rid myself of that terrible thought, a feeling of tragedy over shadowed my previous joyous mood. I noticed a strange man standing in the corner of the room with a little girl hovering close beside him; she had beautiful long black curls reaching down to her tiny waist.

I went over and introduced myself thinking that he must be someone's son or grandson who obviously felt out of place. He looked back at me with such relief to be noticed, even to be spoken to, that I felt ashamed that I hadn't noticed him earlier.

His huge brown eyes carried a sadness and regret that touched me deeply right away. "My name is Joseph," he said, "and this is my daughter, Christiana. We haven't been here for several months because my wife was very sick. She died three weeks ago."

Immediately, I knew the significance of the manger scene. All along I had been praying for this family and his wife. It was odd that I hadn't heard their names mentioned at church, but I had been pleading for them without knowing it. Now, amidst all the confusion, watching the merriment of the children eating their cookies and opening their tiny presents, listening to the tapes of Christmas carols, I knew what to say and how to help these two hurt people. God had prepared me for this moment. He had even filled me with remorse for their situation before I ever knew them.

I could never fill their loss, but my sympathy and caring brought them some comfort on the night of Christ's birth, a time when we want to feel closest to the ones we love and to our Lord.

I've never found a replacement for Mary. I did find a set of three figurines that matched mine on sale after Christmas. The new Mary resembles the others almost perfectly. But I still have a Joseph and baby that I can't bear to leave in the closet. They sit on the side table still by themselves. I suppose every blessing occurs in God's good time.

Joseph has bought a house, a place large enough to include his parents. But he still hasn't found a wife, a replacement for his Stella.

ZEKE WILLIAMS AT THE RILEY-WILLIAMS HOUSE

THE RILEY-WILLIAMS HOUSE
1904
EATONTON, GEORGIA

The 1904 turn-of-the-century Victorian home with a huge veranda was built by Gayle K. Riley, a cotton factor. The Rileys lived in the home until the late 1920s when the boll weevil struck down the cotton industry. Between the 1930s and the 1960s, the home was divided up into two apartments and rented out.

When the Williamses bought the Riley home, a great deal of remodeling was necessary to remove the apartment partitions and redecorate. From the beginning, Carol Williams noticed a great deal of creaking, bumping and groaning that seemed out of the ordinary even for an old house like this one. Several times it sounded as if someone were walking down the hall in high heels, but when she investigated, she found the front of the house empty. Sometimes the footsteps occurred in the afternoon, and at other times the clap, clap, clap of high heels resounded in the hall at dusk. The house was always empty at the time. After the phenomena occurred too many times, Carol became suspicious and wondered whether there had been a ghost in the house.

Former residents of one of the apartments asked the Williamses if they had noticed any strange noises. Carol and Zeke, her husband, were surprised by the question and were more than happy to confess their experiences. The former residents had also heard the footsteps and other noises and were eager to tell their tales as well. The former residents thought it was the spirit of an elderly woman who had died in a fire in the other apartment in the fifties. Other residents had told them that the woman was in the habit of getting up during the night and walking to the kitchen to get a drink, some thought alcohol. The former residents agreed that the footsteps sounded exactly the same after the old woman died.

FRONT BEDROOM

When the Williams daughter's boyfriend was visiting from Scotland, he stayed in the guest room downstairs next to the front hall. One night the daughter and her friend were sitting on the huge Victorian bed when a great gust of freezing air passed by them and a fanny-like depression occurred on the other side of the bed. They were so startled that they jumped up and ran out of the room, not wanting to return.

One afternoon not long after that episode, Carol and Zeke were telling a friend about the experience while they were all standing in the hall, just outside of the bedroom. The friend laughed nervously and exclaimed, "You don't believe in ghosts do you?"

No sooner were the words out of her mouth when the sparkling, cut glass, four-inch-long crystals on the green Hurricane lamp hanging from the ceiling in the center of the hall began to sway in one direction as if a hand were passing by and pushing each one up and letting it fall back down. This phenomena occurred until all the crystals surrounding the lamp were in continuous motion. All the witnesses became spellbound by the movement and didn't say a word until all the crystals had stopped moving. The observers were still so stunned by the antic, obviously from a spirit, that nothing seemed to be the same in the house for the rest of that week. No one mentioned the incident, evidently afraid they might generate further activity. The spirit did seem to be lighthearted though.

THE PSYCHIC

Several weeks later a psychic was brought over by a neighbor. Before they arrived, Carol made up the bed in the front bedroom and straightened up after her house guests. After hearing all the stories, the psychic wanted to go into the guest bedroom to see for herself. She sensed a presence and thought it was a lady, perhaps the former owner, Mrs. Riley.

Later that day after the psychic left, Carol found all the pillows on the bed disheveled and scattered as if someone had messed them up. She knew for sure that no one had been in there after the psychic, and she always left the room neat.

MRS. RILEY'S DAUGHTER

When Mrs. Riley's daughter visited the house in 1980, she was surprised to see that the furniture in the guest room was positioned exactly as her mother had placed it. The head of the Victorian bed was placed in the far corner of the room instead of against the flat wall. Even the marble top wash stand next to the closet was exactly as Mrs. Riley had decorated. At the foot of the bed the curved velvet Victorian chaise was almost identical to the one Mrs. Riley had owned. The daughter couldn't get over the coincidence. Even the wall paper closely resembled the large rose design that Mrs. Riley chose. Later, another psychic thought that maybe Mrs. Riley's spirit influenced Carol's choice of furniture.

DUNCAN'S VISION

In 1992 Zeke's father's sister, Aunt Mayce, visited the Williamses to celebrate her birthday. During Aunt Mayce's birthday party, Duncan, the son of Carol and Zeke Williams, witnessed the white apparition of a woman enter the front hall and walk into the dinning room. Amazed by what he saw, Duncan followed the spirit just in time to watch it vanish near the door. It happened so quickly that he was overcome with astonishment. Duncan didn't recognize the vision or hear or smell anything unusual. He has never seen the woman since.

No one knows for sure who the spirits in the house are because several people died in the house. But the Williamses believe that the spirits are good natured and definitely posses a fine sense of humor. Now when anything occurs, the family is still surprised, but the antics are taken lightly, because they feel that no harm is intended.

DEMOSTHENIAN HALL
UNIVERSITY OF GEORGIA
ATHENS, GEORGIA

There is a legend that is associated with a huge oak tree that once grew between Demosthenian Hall and the chapel next door. A young lad named Robert Toombs (1810-1885) was dismissed from Franklin College in 1828 because of his "boisterous" activity. Five decades later he returned to the college campus on the next commencement day after the anniversary of his dismissal. He stood under the oak tree and delivered an address so lovely and so eloquent in manner that an audience in the church next door couldn't ignore him and en masse came out to hear what the gentleman had to say.

In the years after his untimely dismissal, Robert Toombs was to distinguish himself as a lawyer, planter and statesman. He served the Georgia Legislature as a member of the House of Representatives (1837-1840), (1842-1845); the United States Congress (1845-1853); and the United States Senate (1853-1861). After the secession of the South from the Union, Robert Toombs served the Confederacy as Secretary of State and Brigadier General of the Confederate States of America. In 1877 he served on Georgia's Constitutional Convention.

On the day he died, the oak tree next to the chapel was struck by lightning and ultimately died in 1908. When the tree was taken down, the pieces were cut up and given as commemorative mementoes to alumni. One large piece was placed in the center yard of Demosthenian Hall. In past years it has been a tradition

DEMOSTHENIAN HALL

for anyone who was running for office to stand on the stump for good luck and give his address to the public.

Over the years though, many students have witnessed the apparition of a Confederate officer who appears in and around Demosthenian Hall. Many think it is the spirit of Robert Toombs, who for some unknown reason is compelled to return to this place. Maybe it is because he suffered disgrace in his early years and has striven to over come this deficit all his life. Or maybe he is trying to right an unjust wrong. Whatever the reason, a marker stands on the spot where the oak tree grew and where he gave his eloquent speech, to pay homage to his life as a statesman and remember his death. It was placed there by the direction of the General Assembly and approved in 1985.

The Hall is now used by the Literary Society and as a brides room for marriages in the chapel.

MIDWAY, GEORGIA

Spirits still roam the cemetery in the crossroads town of Midway, Georgia, a community established in 1752 by Puritan settlers. Echoes of their folklore whisper from the soft breezes that weave their way through the gray moss hanging from the three-century-year-old oaks. The stories are repeated over and over again as each visitor, searching for touches of the Old South, meanders through the museum and cemetery. Here they are never disappointed because the tales are as varied, true and peculiar as were the first Puritan settlers of Midway.

Midway Congregational Church is one of Georgia's historical landmarks and over the years has been established as a symbol of the New England influence on southern society. The town was founded by the forty-four original settlers immigrating from Dorchester, Connecticut, and Dorchester, South Carolina. They obtained a 22,700 acre land grant from Savannah in July 1752, and twenty-eight others received 9,650 acres, making a total of 31,950 acres in all. Every family who settled in the Midway community brought with them their own Negro slaves, and when the community was fully established, the population consisted of 250 whites and 1,500 Negroes.

After a few years the planters built summer homes in Sunbury, a province only nine miles away on the Atlantic coast. They found the area near the ocean to be a healthier climate because of the salt water and sea air, and the settlers eventually gave up their winter plantation homes further inland. Most of the plantations grew rice in the low swamplands and other crops like cotton and indigo on the higher ground. But the swamps bred mosquitoes, which carried the diseases of yellow fever and malaria that caused many deaths among the white settler families and black slaves. Some of the Negroes were immune to these diseases, however, because they carried what is known as the sickle cell trait in their red blood cells and were, therefore, prevented from contracting the disease. Unfortunately, this trait made heirs susceptible to sickle cell anemia, also a fatal disease. Those not immune to the fevers died in great numbers. As the years passed, most of the settlers moved to the coast, leaving the plantations deep in middle Georgia in the care of overseers.

The original settlers of Midway returned from Sunbury to the Midway Congregational Church for religious services every Sunday. The trip from Sunbury was tolerable, from other locations maybe twelve or fifteen miles. Near the church, families built pavilions, which they called arbors, so they might have shelter to refresh themselves between the long services and before their trip home.

The Puritans placed a high value on education and set high standards for their children. From among these first owners came the founders of the first Georgia Legislature. Lyman Hall, Button Gwinnett and John Elliott signed the Declaration of Independence for Georgia. Five counties in Georgia—Screven, Hall, Gwinnett, Baker and Stewart—were named for Midway men.

When the Yankees invaded Midway in 1864, they destroyed all the plantations and freed the slaves. A barren land followed, which led to a great poverty of the entire South Georgia area. Kilpatrick's cavalry division encamped for six weeks on Midway church grounds. The cornerstone of the church was opened and rifled of its contents. Sherman penned his horses and cattle in the church yard, used the church as a slaughter house and the melodeon as a meat block. The country was overrun by thousands

MIDWAY SOCIETY MUSEUM

of freed slaves who did not know what to do with their new freedom. There was no hope of regaining the economy because the white people couldn't cultivate the rice and cotton fields by themselves and they couldn't afford to pay the blacks to work.

The last annual meeting of the Midway Society was held in December 1865. This society had always been closed to outsiders. No one was ever allowed to move in unless voted on and approved by all. To this day the Midway Congregational Church and the Midway Society Museum are funded by contributions held in trust from members of the original society and aided with the help of state funds.

THE GRAVE OF JOHN LAMBERT

JOHN LAMBERT
MIDWAY, GEORGIA

The ancient cemetery across the street from the Midway Congregational Church is reminiscent of how we picture the Old South. Three-hundred-year-old, moss-draped, live oaks shade the graves of the long dead patriots but can't stop the occasional disturbance from a vagrant spirit. Just to the left of the wrought-iron front gate stands a magnificent marble monument erected to the memory of John Lambert, a resident who died in 1786. Carved on two sides of the four-sided seven-foot pillar are the likenesses of needy women gathering in their children. The pictures of needy women and children illustrate some of the chapters in the life of John Lambert.

On a cold winter night in the late 1700s, an old man and woman were crossing a bridge in South Carolina on their way home from church when they heard the cry of a baby. Immediately, they stopped their carriage. In a basket under the shelter of the bridge, they found a white baby boy, screaming his lungs out, evidently abandoned by his mother. The couple took the baby home to Midway and raised him as their own, calling him John Lambert, after the name of the Lambert Bridge where they discovered him.

John Lambert's foster parents died when he was only a young child, and he was again left orphaned and penniless. But the people of the town took pity on him and vowed to raise him in a Christian manner until he was almost a grown man. So each of the planters of the neighborhood decided to take him into their family for one year at a time to feed, clothe and educate him.

One day while digging in a swamp, John Lambert discovered a rare piece of Indian pottery. This discovery was the beginning of his good fortune. He traded the jug for a hen and entered into the chicken business; from his chicken profits he invested in pigs and then cows. After several years of good fortune, he was able to buy a mule and a Negro slave; finally, he obtained a land grant. His fortunes increased rapidly, and soon he was able to move into the Midway community, as a man of "no small means." John Lambert became one of Midway's most highly respected citizens and served three times on the board of select men. But even though he made a name and fortune for himself, he never married. The members of the Midway community married their daughters only to gentry, and because Lambert's origins were unknown, he was not an approved suitor. Unfortunately, his future was dictated by the rules of the strict Puritan society.

Lambert subsequently bequeathed his extensive estate and land holdings in trust to the Midway Congregational Church. His bequest stated that it be used for charitable purposes and for the promotion and provision of learning and religious salvation for those less fortunate. For nearly one-hundred-fifty years, this estate has been a wonderful help to the needy, both black and white, and has assisted in the support of the three Presbyterian Churches in the county.

Even though the funds have been depleted over the years, they are still part of the churches' endowment today. Without this money, the Midway Congregational Church and Museum might have disappeared years ago.

A PATRIOTIC COW
MIDWAY, GEORGIA

Late one evening in 1778, Amanda ——— was sitting in the barnyard milking her cow. She heard the muffled sounds of voices coming from the meeting house down the street. When she stood up to investigate the commotion, she discovered two of General Provost's men setting fire to the building. She waited for them to disappear before racing toward the flames with her bucket of fresh milk. She was just in time and extinguished completely the rapidly spreading flames, saving the church from certain destruction.

After making certain that the fire was completely out, she returned to her milking and hoped the cow would cooperate.

Later that evening, the soldiers returned and rekindled the fire. When Amanda spotted the spiraling black smoke and the new flames, she was horrified. Without a second's hesitation she charged out the back door and carried her new bucket of fresh milk with her to the fire. She proved again to be a very efficient fire department.

The third time the fire was set, the flames raged too long before they were discovered, and the milk supply had given out. Unfortunately, the church burned to the ground. Strange to say, no monument has been erected to the cow.

BRICK GRAVE LIFTED BY OAK TREE

THE SUICIDE
MIDWAY, GEORGIA

Only one of the members of the Midway Society ever committed suicide. According to reports, he was a handsome and gallant youth who had a double attack of the treacherous disease, heart and love sickness. He fell madly in love with two young ladies at the same time. One was so good and clever that he couldn't resist her, and the other was so beautiful that he couldn't take his eyes off her. One moment he worshipped one, and the next moment with equal fervor he worshipped the other. He was overcome with anguish, and his heart was torn from this unbearable conflict. He was unable to decide which one he loved the most and knew in his heart that he couldn't have both.

The situation haunted him day and night and overcame him, paralyzing him as surely as if an evil spell had been cast upon him. He couldn't think, he couldn't eat, he couldn't conduct business—he was overwhelmed with grief. The young man could bear it no longer and took his own life.

The Puritans did not believe that a suicide victim should be given a Christian burial. So the unfortunate, love-struck young man was buried in disgrace under a big oak tree just outside the brick wall of Midway Cemetery.

Some years later the wall of the graveyard was moved and extended beyond the large oak tree to increase the inside area so that more families might be included. Thereafter, the unfortunate young man's grave was inside the wall, and he was honored as one buried among the distinguished citizens of Midway. Some say that the spirits took pity on him, forgiving his disgrace and giving him a place of honor among the dead.

As the years passed though, the oak tree grew in size, creating a huge root system. As the body of the extended roots surrounded the large brick tomb, it was lifted up out of the earth, maybe as an offering to the almighty, or maybe in an attempt to flee the too pious cemetery. It is still there for all to see. You be the judge.

THE CRACK IN THE WALL
MIDWAY, GEORGIA

People claim that there has always been a crack in the north wall of the cemetery, just beyond the grave of the suicide victim. Some think the crack is due to the shifting of the earth; others conclude that the crack is from the invading tree roots of the giant oak only several feet away, but the truth remains a mystery to this day.

The extended brick wall of the cemetery was built by Negro slaves, each planter furnishing his share of the labor. One day two of the slaves quarreled and failed to finish their stint. In the late afternoon the overseer sent all the others home, but left these two to complete their task. The two continued to argue long into the afternoon, until one couldn't contain his rage and attacked the other with a brick, brutally bashing the man to death. In a fevered frenzy the surviving slave tore down the brick wall and buried his partner under the foundation. The slave worked hastily and long into the night, trying to rebuild the wall before the overseer returned.

After finishing the brick wall by moonlight, the slave returned home to his plantation and claimed the other slave had run away. The brick wall began to crumble as quickly as it was built, and no manner of repair could rectify the situation. Finally, the wall was completely dismantled and every brick removed all the way down to the foundation. Deep in the trench, they uncovered the bones of the murdered Negro.

THE CRACK IN THE WALL

Satisfied that the cause of the crumbling wall had been found, Midway residents ordered the slaves to replace the wall just as it had been built originally. But according to the old Negroes, "Ain't no use fer de white folks fer men' um. Dat nigger haint gwine crack um fas'es it git fix."

Today, the crack in the wall begins deep in the foundation and rises up, twisting and turning around each brick until it reaches the wall's full height and moves cleanly across the top, no matter how many times the wall is repaired.

CHLOE
MIDWAY, GEORGIA

Located in the center of the Midway Cemetery are four raised brick graves, the last resting place of the four wives of William ———. The inscriptions carved in each marble slab indicate that three of his wives died young. Here is the story of their early and tragic deaths:

Master William owned a young mulatto girl named Chloe who had been imported on a boat from the North and sold at Sunbury. No one knew anything about her past, but she considered herself superior to the other Negroes on his plantation. The beautiful young girl appeared to be properly trained and quickly became a house servant, but she made too many mistakes and the angry mistress sent her out of the house to work in the rice fields. Very soon after Chloe began her backbreaking toil, the mistress became ill and suddenly died of unexplained causes.

In only a few days Chloe pleaded with the Mas and reestablished herself as a servant in the plantation house. Although Hannah, Mas William's faithful old maumer, became distressed at Chloe's presence in the big house, Chloe had somehow endeared herself to the Mas, and no amount of persuasion could change his mind.

In the early 1800s when a man lost his wife, he was encouraged to take another. Death among the young was not uncommon because medical care was mostly absent. After a year of mourning, Mas William brought home another bride. Chloe had lived in the big house for a whole year, having her own way,

THE GRAVES OF MAS WILLIAM'S FOUR WIVES

so she resented the intrusion of this new wife. The new wife complained that Chloe disobeyed her orders and created quarrels among the other staff.

Maumer Hannah declared, "Dat gal t'ink she white. Dat wher meck um so uppety."

At last the master told Chloe he could tolerate her behavior no longer. She would go back to the fields, and if she didn't behave there, she would be sold. The next day the master was too distressed and anxious to think of Chloe, for his wife was desperately ill. In a few hours she mysteriously passed away.

The master became very lonely without a mistress. Hannah rejoiced when she observed that the Mas William, "Lif' he eye frum de groun' an' sta't fer look roun'."

But trouble still lurked on the plantation. The third mistress lived only a few years. Mum Hannah grew to despise and distrust Chloe, claiming that there was something wicked about the girl. She snooped around the house when she had no business there. Some of the Negroes were even a little afraid of her, declaring that she "tote p'ison."

Mas William was very depressed, but for the fourth time he took a bride. When guests called in the evening after the wedding, Chloe served the wine. Someone proposed a toast. The bride and groom exchanged glasses and raised them to their lips. Darting forward, Chloe knocked the glass from her master's hand, gasping, "That glass ain't for you!"

With an exclamation of terror, she snatched from her dress a black vial, drank its contents and fled, crying "Chloe is gone— gone!" The evil mulatto girl died instantly in the same manner as Mas William's other three wives. The mystery surrounding their death finally became clear. Adding to Mas William's great sorrow, he realized that Chloe had poisoned them all.

Mas William's wives are buried in the Midway Cemetery.

SYLVIA AND HER LOVER
MIDWAY CEMETERY
MIDWAY, GEORGIA

Two young spellbound lovers met secretly every night at
midnight in the Midway Cemetery, hoping that no one would
ever discover them there. They hid in the farthest corner so that
even if a visitor happened to enter the brick-walled sanctuary in
the early hours of the morning, the two could steal away unnoticed.
Unlike most couples of that day, these two were destined for
tragedy because they could never receive consent from friends,
family or even society for their marriage. They were even more
cursed than the fated Romeo and Juliet: the man wasn't considered
by society to be the young girl's social equal because the man,
Anthony, was a black slave and Sylvia was the pure-white
daughter of a wealthy planter.

Weeks turned into months, and Sylvia's parents began talking
of marriage for their beautiful, wealthy daughter. They mentioned
all the handsome, eligible suitors from Midway and surrounding
areas that might have caught her fancy at the balls and parties
that she had attended. But no one raised a spark of interest in the
girl. In fact, she ignored all their suggestions and changed the
subject immediately. Finally, she could stand the predicament
no longer and, out of the blue, confessed that she had a secret
lover.

Sylvia watched with dismay as her parent's excitement grew,
and she kept postponing their fated meeting of Anthony. But as
the weeks passed, having them wait any longer became difficult.

One afternoon Anthony came to her home and knocked at the front door. Her father acted insulted at the sight of the black man and told him to go around to the back because blacks were never permitted to enter a white person's home by the front door.

With her heart in her throat, Sylvia grabbed Anthony's arm as he was about to leave and turned to face her confused father.

"Father, this is Anthony. He is the man I want to marry," Sylvia said softly. She wasn't prepared for her father's tyrannical reaction.

Hysteria gripped Sylvia's father, and he lunged toward the black man's throat, choking him with a vengeance and claiming that Anthony had defiled his precious only daughter. Her mother screamed and fainted as Anthony was being dragged away.

Crying uncontrollably, Sylvia was locked in her room and forbidden to leave the house or to ever see Anthony again until a proper marriage could be arranged with someone else. The next day Sylvia's father arrived with a suitor for his daughter to marry, a man who had been asking for Sylvia's hand for months, but Sylvia loathed and despised him. Knowing that he was only after her money, she had refused his attentions all along. When she saw the man her father intended for her to marry, she refused to come to meet him; still the wedding was set for the very next day. In those days marriages were arranged many times for financial reasons, not for love.

Sylvia cried herself to sleep and woke up in the wee hours of the morning. She climbed out of the window and jumped to the ground below, spraining her ankle. But she didn't care and limped and ran through the forest and the fields as fast as she could to the cemetery, hoping to find Anthony there. When she reached the brick wall, her arms and legs were scratched and bleeding from briers and low hanging branches, but she didn't care. All she could think of was her precious Anthony. After searching and searching the low bushes where they often met and whispering his name, she reached their corner to find it empty. She stood out in the open where the moonlight shone brightly through the trees, and still calling his name, she looked up just in time to see the moon slide behind a cloud. When the moon became visible again, she saw her Anthony, hanging from the huge limb of the live oak tree. Filled with anguish, Sylvia pulled Anthony's body to the ground. He was stabbed through the heart, and when she tried to pull out the knife, she saw the note from her father which said:

>   Sylvia,
>   I told you to stay away from this blank, blank, blank. If you aren't going to obey me, then I will make you obey.

She placed the note over her own heart and pressed the knife into it as hard as she could until it reached its target, her own heart.

The next day the caretaker found them both dead, lying in each others arms, in the far corner of the cemetery. For years afterwards different people claimed to have seen an apparition of the entwined lovers sitting under the tree where their bodies had fallen even though their bodies had been buried outside the cemetery wall, rejected because of their crimes.

A CHILD GHOST
MIDWAY, GEORGIA

An unnamed six-year-old child was crossing the street at a Midway crossroads when she was struck by a truck and killed instantly.

Soon after the accident, several residents of the town witnessed the appearance of the apparition of the young girl not far from where she was killed. A couple living in a house near the site of the tragic accident saw the ghost of the child walk in front of their television one night. The couple was so frightened that they couldn't move an inch. The child walked to the door, turned, looked sadly back at the couple and then departed.

A neighbor was driving home late one night and saw the apparition of the young girl standing in the middle of his lane of traffic. He didn't realize that the child was a ghost, and he swerved to miss hitting her. He lost control of his automobile and ran off the road into the ditch. The ghost girl disappeared from sight. He got out of his car to search for her and was amazed as he watched another automobile speed down the wrong side of the road. If he had still been on the road, the automobile driven by a drunken driver would have hit him head on. The apparition of the ghost-girl had saved his life.

THE COGDELL LIGHT
COGDELL, GEORGIA

In the tiny town of Cogdell, Georgia, at the beginning of the War Between the States, the owner of a large plantation decided to join the army of the Confederacy. Thinking that the war wouldn't last more than two or three weeks, the owner instructed his long trusted and faithful servant to wait for his return every night at the crossroads with a lantern.

Just as instructed, after two weeks time, the servant waited at the crossroads with a lantern to guide his master across the swamp and over the precarious roads to the plantation. The servant waited for four long years without seeing his master. When the war ended, the owner still hadn't returned. The servant discovered that the owner had been reported missing in action. The trusted servant refused to believe that his owner was dead and continued his watch at the crossroads just in case the man might return.

The weeks turned into years, and after thirty years of waiting every night at the crossroads, the trusted servant died. Many years have passed and the town has disappeared, leaving only the crossing of the roads, overgrown forests, and black cypress swamps. But hundreds of people passing through this area on dark nights have witnessed a light hovering at the crossroads. Some people claim that the light is the illumination from the swamp gas common in the area. Others swear that the light is the spirit of the long trusted servant who returns nightly to the crossroads to light the way for his master.

THE GHOSTS OF CUMBERLAND ISLAND
CUMBERLAND ISLAND, GEORGIA

Cumberland Island is one of Georgia's best kept secrets. The ever changing barrier island lies just off the coast of the tiny antebellum town of St. Mary's, Georgia. Ranging wild horses and white tailed deer graze amid mysterious moss-laden walls and chimneys, remnants of the 1890s Carnegie mansion, the ruins of Dungeness.

Miles of live oaks grown together provide a canopy shelter from the hot sun for visitors and animals alike. Armadillo and alligators are often stumbled upon by visitors while walking along the cushioned leaf strewn paths. The great Loggerhead turtle still migrates back to Cumberland's brilliant hot sand beaches every summer to nest, just as it has for the last thousand years. Now most of the island is owned by the National Park Service and is open to the public for hiking and primitive camping experiences. Because the only access is by ferry from St. Marys, the island maintains its wilderness state.

Since 1884 when the great steel tycoon, Thomas Carnegie, built a small retreat on Cumberland Island, five generations of the Carnegie family have been so bewitched by the interminable peace and natural charm of the place that they spent their winters there. Many family members stayed the summers, too, and ultimately raised their children in the controlled and protected atmosphere of Cumberland's wilderness. The salt marshes, woodland paths and deserted beaches became a Shangri-La from the industrialized, steel-producing Pittsburgh, where the Carnegies

DUNGENESS BEFORE FIRE

THE STAFFORD HOUSE

created a financial empire. Now more than a century later, these same Carnegies have found their last resting place in the family cemetery plot, shaded forever beneath the sheltering arms of the moss-laden live oaks.

In 1972 in order to preserve the island as a natural habitat and prevent further developing, the family sold all its holdings but thirteen-hundred acres to the National Park Service. Grayfield, one of the original Carnegie mansions, was retained by one branch of the family and converted to an inn.

Many say that the island is haunted. Several people have died there, and ever since, stories have been passed around about the spirits who have stayed behind. It's no wonder that they stayed because the wild beauty of the place immediately haunts visitors. The mysterious ruins and the other abandoned Carnegie mansions situated in different locations on the island invite speculation. They belong to the park service now, but they still haunt the imagination with questions of what happened and how they became castoffs, abandoned sand castles on a great beach.

In 1993 Nancy Carnegie Rockefeller wrote her personal memoirs into a book for the family and titled it *The Carnegies and Cumberland Island*.

The following anecdotes are stories from that collection of family memories.

THE STAFFORD HOUSE

When Uncle Bill (William Coleman Carnegie) married Aunt Gertrude (Gertrude Ely from Cleveland, Ohio), a beautiful and loving, fine-featured woman with a regal posture, Mama Carnegie (Lucy) gave them the old Stafford Plantation House on Cumberland Island to live in. It is located five miles north on the main road from Dungeness and had been Robert Stafford's home on his cotton plantation before the War Between the States. The white frame plantation house was surrounded by a waist high Tabby wall which is still there.

One quiet Sunday afternoon in the late 1890s, while all the women in the family were sitting on the front porch gossiping, the original house caught fire and quickly burned to the ground. No one ever said how the fire started, but Aunt Gertrude was one of the women sitting with the others, while the men were off playing golf.

At the first sight of smoke, everyone panicked and raced into the house, trying to save what they could grab. China and furniture were thrown out the windows and pillows were carefully carried out as if they were breakable—every one was in such a tizzy. The fire raged out of control, and in the span of an hour's time, the once beautiful two-story house had been reduced to ashes.

One man carried out the bronze bust of a man wearing a tall silk hat and playing a guitar. Ordinarily, this statue would have been too heavy for one man to carry alone. Nancy also heard that Aunt Gertrude insisted on going to the second floor to get the "rat of hair" she usually wore in her pompadour to keep her hair in place.

Aunt Gertrude and Uncle Bill moved into the small Tabby House nearby until their new home was completed. Later a pool was added to the old Tabby House, and at one time it was turned into a golf house.

The island became a winter haven for the family and their guests for "the season." They fished for channel crabs and dug for oysters in the canals of the salt marshes, golfed on their new golf course designed by a Scotsman, Thomas Hutchinson, and played tennis and polo. The stables were filled with horses, and Gertrude and Bill often passed the day just riding their thoroughbreds on the beach for pleasure.

According to a story told by Aunt Lucy Ferguson, in March of 1906 everyone visiting Dungeness became very ill with Typhoid fever. George Carnegie thought they got the bug from eating oysters. All had been sick for days when Aunt Gertrude died unexpectedly of other causes.

For many years Uncle Bill and Aunt Gertrude had been trying to have a baby. Finally, Aunt Gertrude thought that she was with child. Her stomach grew very large, and many concluded that she must have had cancer because she never delivered. During the Typhoid epidemic, Aunt Gertrude died suddenly in the middle of the night.

Uncle Bill was so distraught when he found her that he didn't know what to do. It had only been a month since her thirty-fifth birthday; how could she be dead? He didn't want to tell the relatives at Dungeness because he feared they were too sick to bear the news and it might kill them. So in the depths of his despair, he cut off her beautiful long blond braid of hair to save; he carried it with him wherever he went for the rest of his life. He wrapped her body with a shroud, and with the help of his yard man, he carried her outside and buried her in the ground behind Stafford House. But by the time he woke up the next morning, he had come to his senses and realized what had happened. He could barely live with the terrible thing he did, burying his beloved Gertrude without a funeral. So he and the yard man immediately dug her up and brought her body to the house for a proper wake.

For many years after, Uncle Bill mourned his beloved Gertrude's death. Finally, just before his mother's death, he married Betty, the nurse who had cared for him during his depressed years. But not long afterwards, Betty committed suicide, leaving Uncle Bill alone again. He visited Cumberland Island often and at his death was buried there next to his beloved

Gertrude in the Stafford Plot, where he had always longed to be.

William Coleman Carnegie
(Born April 24, 1867 - Died July 28, 1944)
Gertrude Ely Carnegie
(Born February 25, 1871 - Died March 26, 1906)

THE SPIRIT OF STAFFORD HOUSE

The family claims that ever since the day Aunt Gertrude died very mysteriously, unexplainable things have occurred at Stafford and have been witnessed by many of the children and their visitors. These peculiar things happened so often that the family concluded they were the humorous antics of a spirit whom they ultimately named Aunt Gertrude. They were never afraid because they all loved Aunt Gertrude so much.

Whenever the family stayed at Stafford and went out for a picnic, the car broke down on the way back, and they had to walk the entire way home, sometimes several miles. This happened so frequently that eventually members of the party expected it as part of the trip.

Even though the family would leave the house dark, without lights turned on, when they returned to Stafford, it was always blazing with every light fixture glowing, even on the brightest afternoons. The family attributed these odd occurrences to the spirit of Aunt Gertrude, who they claim was still taking care of the house for the family.

Aunt Gertrude also appeared to be a poltergeist, moving things, breaking things, rattling things and acting out often. Many visitors also confessed that their jewelry was misplaced. They swore that they had carefully laid it out on the table, and when they returned to the spot to put it on, the pieces had been moved around—out of place; sometimes they thought it lost completely, but later found it in another location.

AUNT GERTRUDE'S APPARITION

When the family used the little Tabby house nearby as a guest house, it seemed as if her spirit was stronger there than anywhere else. Someone in the family saw her apparition appear once, and ever since, they thought of Aunt Gertrude when something odd happened. She rattled things and made the shades go up and even broke things. The family didn't mind because they had all loved her. Sometimes her antics just made them laugh.

THE POLO PLAYER

In the late 1800s the mansion, Dungeness, was built by Lucy and Thomas Carnegie, brother of the financier, Andrew Carnegie. Lucy became a widow early: Thomas died only two years after the completion of Dungeness. But with six sons to raise, Lucy decided to live at Cumberland Island in the mansion year round. In the 1950s the mansion was destroyed by fire. The walls are disintegrating slowly beneath the towering brick chimneys and have formed upon the landscape an eery, if not foreboding, spectacle. Some say this dwelling is also residence to a ghost who appears to strangers.

During a party one night, a polo player abruptly decided to leave. Some speculate that he was on an errand to fetch more wine for the guests; others say that he left in an angry fury and bolted away before anyone could catch up with him. That same evening, racing his horse across the moonlit beach, he hit a low hanging tree branch and was accidentally knocked out of his

RUINS AT DUNGENESS

saddle. Some believe he may have lay unconscious for several days before he was found. His body was discovered by visitors, but, unfortunately, by then he was dead.

Some people think the polo player was Scotsman Thomas Hutchinson, the man who designed the golf course near Stafford. Unfortunately, he was also killed from falling off a horse and was buried in the Stafford cemetery next to Mr. Stafford. Others don't know for sure who the ghost is.

Sheila Willis, a volunteer who worked on the island, claimed that people still see him or his apparition. Willis, of Waycross, Georgia, glimpsed the phantom in 1991 while working in the servant's quarters:

> "I glanced out of the corner of my eye and saw a bearded man with a white shirt and dark pants walking down the stairs. All of a sudden, I realized he was making no sound at all. No footsteps or anything. I looked back, and he was gone."

Occasionally, in the spring of the year, visitors to the island have witnessed a strange man walking along the road, or sometimes he has appeared to them from out of nowhere. When they speak to him, he disappears. The reports of his sightings have been told many times by different people. He catches them by surprise, and they don't remember seeing him in their group on the ferry. They always inquire about the identity of the stranger.

THE OWLS AT DUNGENESS

In the early '80s when Joe Peacock, a maintenance foreman for the Sanitation Department on Cumberland Island, had been working late, he passed by the ruins of Dungeness on his way home. There were times, he admitted, when the sights raised the hair on the back of his neck, and not much scares him. In the fall of the year when the temperature dropped and there was a full moon, owls congregated at the Dungeness ruins. Five or six would be sitting on top of the chimneys, silhouetted black against the white light of the full moon, calling out into the darkness, "Whoo! Whoo! Whoo!" It was the strangest sight he ever saw. But he hasn't heard them, now that he thinks of it, for several years. Was it an omen or curse? Were they prompted by the spirits of long dead souls congregating for their monthly meeting? He often wondered if there was a reason for their monthly rendezvous.

PLUM ORCHARD

Plum Orchard is the largest of six mansions built by the Carnegies on Cumberland and resembles the White House in style and length, although it is somewhat smaller. Lucy Carnegie built the mansion in 1898 for her son George and his bride, Margaret Thaw. The other Carnegie mansions were built by Lucy Coleman Carnegie for herself and her children.

Even though Plum Orchard was the site of family tragedy (George died in his forties of multiple sclerosis), it was also the site of many happy family gatherings. Nancy and her sister were married there. Their mother returned to Plum Orchard a month ahead and opened the long deserted mansion, scrubbed and cleaned windows, floors and furniture, prepared the gardens with the help of their trusted servants and amassed enough food for over a hundred guests for the three day stay. The girls couldn't imagine being married anywhere else; Plum Orchard had been their childhood home.

After George died, the Johnstons bought the mansion, wanting to preserve the place where they had experienced so many happy moments as visitors.

Coleman Johnston recalled:

> "The only sound at the vacant white stucco Georgian mansion is the flapping of a diving owl protecting his nest atop a two-story column at the main entrance. Bits of his dinner—fur and tiny bones litter the wide porch.
>
> " At dusk the island comes alive with the island sounds. Insects and tree frogs rock the quiet with their humming. Snowy egrets and herons by the hundreds ca-rakk all night from the wax myrtle bushes around Plum Orchard Pond.
>
> "Cumberland is still a vast grazing ground for wild horses, a mixture of mustangs, thoroughbred stallions and Appaloosas, but the cattle now are fenced on private property. We had our own rodeos, managed by my father. We would break the wild mustangs and match them with a thoroughbred stallion my father brought from Kentucky. All the children on the island had ponies. . . ."

In 1972 the mansion was sold to the National Park Service with the other Carnegie holdings and is closed to the public now. But in its prime it boasted an indoor swimming pool, twin Tiffany lamps in the library and an elaborate system of speaking tubes, the annunciators, which communicated requests from the bedrooms to the servants quarters, all reminiscent of the rich and famous of the 1890s-1940s, a lost era.

When a cleaning girl went into a seldom used room at the rear of Plum Orchard, she was overcome by the smell of fresh cigarette smoke, yet, no one else was around. Other times she heard foot steps in the hall, but no one was ever there when she investigated.

Other people have witnessed the appearance of a woman dressed in red in the servants quarters. Some have said that a prostitute died there in the twenties, and ever since, this woman has appeared.

THE WOMAN IN WHITE

The first time Joe Peacock saw the woman in white, something made him glance up at the windows on the second floor of the carriage house on Cumberland Island. This is a two story, hundred-plus-foot long building with a steeply pitched gray roof, and the whole is constructed of tabby concrete, a crushed oyster shell mixture with sand and lime common to the ocean front homes of South Georgia and Florida. Dormer windows line the roof of the eighty-plus-year-old building and give it an old English manor style of architecture. It was March of 1979. He knew that no one had been in that area all morning, so when he saw the white face of a woman with long dark hair peering out of the window, he was amazed and shocked. He knew that no one ever went up there. The area had been used as storage for saddles, bridles and other riding gear that had become outdated. Now the first floor of the carriage house was home to tractors, saws, trailers and other equipment necessary to maintain the island's paths and keep the landscaping in shape. He was bothered that he couldn't make out her features or identify who she was because there weren't many strangers on the island that day.

"Her eyes appeared to be only dark holes in her face. That's when I realized that she must be a ghost," he remarked. "Huge black holes. And this made identifying her even more difficult."

That wasn't the only time he saw her. He spotted her on four different occasions, and each time she appeared a little changed.

Once she was walking past the windows one by one, and he waited and watched for her appearance at the next window. She glanced out of it for only a few seconds and then moved on to the next as a heavy, white, cloudy form that seemed to be blown out of shape by some breeze.

Two other times she seemed to be peering out at something and just stood at the window for a long while without moving before she simply faded away. The forth time he had been looking for her for several days wondering if she might make an appearance. On one afternoon she seemed to be watching him, too; only this time she appeared to be floating up to the full height of the window. When he walked on, she moved to the next window as if she were following him. It gave him shivers up his spine, and he couldn't get her vision out of his head for weeks, he confessed. He imagined her to be rather tall because her head reached the top of the window, exposing her long, wavy white flowing dress. He wondered who she had been and asked many of the residents over the years, but her identity remains a mystery.

Joe was very cautious whom he told about the vision because he didn't want anyone to think he was crazy. But after he confided in several of the other staff members about his sighting of the woman, they confessed that they had seen her also. Evidently, she has been seen by quite a few other people.

No one ever goes up to the second floor of the carriage house anymore. It's an attic where old carriages, harnesses and other paraphernalia associated with the horses are stored; some items date back to the 1890s. The door is always kept locked.

Black Barracks

On another occasion Joe spotted the lady in white when he was standing near a building known as the Black Barracks, located in the cluster of buildings surrounding the Carriage House. About 10 years ago the Black Barracks had a room on the end where the park staff and their families could spend a few days. It was available on a first come first serve basis, and the accommodations were very nice, with hot and cold running water and a small kitchen. The room was occupied quite often by the workers and their families, and it was always in great demand.

He just happened to be walking by the building one afternoon when he witnessed the lady in white again as her white shroud-like apparition passed through the closed door and into that room. She never opened the door but actually passed through it. When he opened the door to see if she was still there, he was not surprised to find the room empty.

THE LEGEND OF JACKSONBOROUGH'S CURSE
SYLVANIA, GEORGIA

In 1821 an itinerant minister named Lorenzo Dow descended like a Jeremiah on the prosperous but lawless town of Jacksonborough, in Screven County, Georgia. The town supported more saloons than homes and had grown rapidly into a flourishing center for pioneers and fur traders. These were men who arrived hungry and thirsty from the wilds of the frontier. Lorenzo Dow traveled from one saloon to another preaching, ". . . the actions of sin are death and with Jesus there is life." He was as persistent as a man dogged by a fiendish phantom and never gave up.

At first he entered the saloons with moral indignation, placing notices on all the walls and announcing his prayer meetings at the local Methodist church. But when the drunkards and rebel-rousers refused to attend his meetings and weren't moved by his eloquent and passionate sermons, Dow used more pointed methods and verbally attacked the sinners' ingestion of alcoholic beverages and love of immoral entertainment.

The men revolted against Dow's persistent assault on their lifestyle, formed an angry mob and vowed to take care of that "hunchbacked little minister."

While Dow was conducting his meeting, the angry saloon crew shouted obscenities at the church and pitched bricks through the windows. They screamed for Dow to show his face as they shot their guns into the air, frightening everyone around. Dow didn't respond to their demands, but merely kept on preaching the gospel inside. Disgusted, the angry crowd left and returned to their saloons. But after the meeting, Dow followed the men and dared to face them—a lone minister against a mob of half-crazy drunkards.

Lorenzo Dow was beaten badly, and just when it looked as if he had spoken his last word, he was rescued by a prominent and moral man, Seaborne Goodall, who served as a clerk of the Superior Court. Goodall dragged Dow out of the saloon; all the time Dow was screaming the resurrection and kicking back at his attackers. Once in the safety of Goodall's home, Dow rested for several weeks, recovering from his injuries. After much persuasion by Mr. Goodall, Dow finally decided to leave town.

While Dow was on his way out of Jacksonbourough, the drunkards heard of his escape and vowed to teach him another lesson. They quickly followed him and pulled him off his horse. Placing him between two boards, they cruelly sat on him, chiding that they were going to straighten his back or send him to the devil. The men didn't know the true power behind the hand of God.

Lorenzo miraculously escaped, and when he reached the Beaver Dam Creek Bridge, he turned and faced the few screaming drunkards who had caught up with him. Taking off his cracked and worn black leather shoes, he shook the dirt of Jacksonborough off of them forever. He cursed the town and asked God to destroy it as completely as God had destroyed Sodom and Gomorrah—with one exception, the Seaborne Goodall house. With that he pulled his black felt hat down over his ears, buttoned his black coat high around his neck, turned his horse away and rode off, never looking back.

Within 30 years the town of Jacksonborough was gone, all except for the Goodall house. Over the years all manner of disaster, fire, tornado, hurricane and mysterious flash floods destroyed all buildings as fast as they could be rebuilt. The people of the town died also of mysterious causes and devastating epidemics, all except the Methodist minister and the owner of the Goodall house. Finally, the Methodist minister, knowing of the curse, tore down the courthouse brick by brick and moved it south six miles. The town of Sylvania soon sprang up and prospered in this new spot. In 1847 Sylvania became the county seat. Today all that remains of Jacksonborough is the home of Seaborne Goodall.

Many people question the existence of Jacksonborough at all or even the life of Lorenzo Dow. Is the legend true? The people of Sylvania say it is, even though there are no records that Jacksonborough ever existed. But in the cemeteries there are many citizens who have been named after Lorenzo Dow as a tribute to his Godliness.

There is one piece of unrefutable evidence, and that is the presence of the restored Seaborne Goodall home, which has become a landmark for the citizens of Sylvania and a reminder of the true power of God. It stands alone at the end of a wide unpaved road, exactly six miles north of Sylvania.

THE SPIRITS OF THE CEMETERY
WADLEY, GEORGIA

Shirley and her daughter, Bonnie, have been researching their family genealogy for the past several years and were visiting a cemetery in Wadley, Georgia, in March of 1996. After spending some time searching the name Watkins among the tombstones and not finding it, they became very discouraged. But suddenly they began to smell the faint aroma of burning incense. As they continued their mission, the fragrance grew stronger and stronger until the air was loaded with it. They looked everywhere for flowers blooming, but found none and realized that March was too early for most blooms.

Shirley had the distinct feeling that someone was there watching them—maybe trying to give them a sign. She intuitively sensed that it was the spirit of an elegant lady, but she never saw her.

Shirley and her daughter returned to the cemetery in June and experienced the same phenomenon; only this time a man pulled up in a station wagon. They were leery about speaking to him because the cemetery was located on a little traveled road in a rural area. But he seemed friendly and asked if he could help them. They told him the name they were looking for, and he offered to check with someone in town. Not long afterwards he returned with a phone number and insisted that they call that person.

When they phoned the unknown number, they discovered that it led them to a second cousin that she had never met and reassured her that they had been absolutely safe the entire time.

A Rising Mist

On another visit to the cemetery near the Tarker Methodist Church, in Louisville, Georgia, Shirley experienced another strange phenomenon. This church and cemetery was deserted also, and the women had to travel down a rural road to get there. She and her daughter searched the tombstones in the high grass but didn't have any luck. Suddenly they saw a white mist appear at the back of the cemetery above the tangled honeysuckle and overgrown saplings. Even though she felt a strong urgency to investigate that area, she was too frightened by the cloud that was still hovering over one of the graves. She was so frightened that she and her daughter left as quickly as they could. She admits that she tries to be cautious when researching the old cemetery because of snakes and ill-meaning prowlers, but Shirley never dreamed that she needed to be wary of spirits.

Shirley had traveled all the way from California to South Georgia to find the locations of some of her family members' graves, and so far she hadn't had much luck. Several days later Shirley and her daughter returned to the cemetery, and to their great relief the mist was gone. Carefully, they picked their way through the overgrowth to the spot where they saw the cloud. Sure enough, after some arduous clearing away of leaves and vines, they found the graves of her Watkins relatives that she had been searching for. They seemed to be in the same location where she saw the cloud a few days before. She knew then that the spirit of her relative was trying to help and not harm her.

ALABAMA

LAVENDER ON THE PILLOW
UNIVERSITY OF ALABAMA
TUSCALOOSA, ALABAMA

When Ann Buchannen Strickland was a coed at the University of Alabama in Tuscaloosa, she searched frantically for just the right apartment near the campus where she would live until the end of the year. She wanted a homey place where she'd be comfortable and be stimulated to study. It was only a couple of days before classes began in January 1983, and she still hadn't found a permanent location. Time was running out, and she knew all the great apartments had been taken. The ones left were either too small, too expensive, too dirty, or too far away from campus.

Late in the afternoon two days before classes started, she had just about given up her search. She was getting frantic wondering what she would do if she couldn't find anything.

She didn't know what made her cut through a narrow alley to the next street, but she almost missed the sign on the lawn of the corner house saying, "For Rent" in bold letters. The house was a rather old turn-of-the-century English Tudor brick type, and this room appeared to be on the second level. So she decided to investigate.

When the old woman let her into the room, Ann was immediately greeted by the stuffy odor of antiquated furniture and a subtle scent of lavender. It was the identical perfume she remembered her great-grandmother wore. The rough plaster walls were painted a pale shade of lavender and looked lovely in the afternoon light from the large French-type windows. It had a tiny kitchen that was very usable and sturdy dark oak Mission style furniture. There was even a desk where she could study. She sat on the bed and seemed to fall into it. This was too good to be true. She felt as if she belonged there. The window unit air conditioner would block out any noise from the street, she thought.

"I'll take it," she finally said to the old woman who owned the house, who admitted that the former tenant had decided at the last minute to move. She had wondered if she'd be able to rent the apartment at that late date.

"I've decided to give you a discount on the rent," she said, smiling, while patting Ann on her shoulder.

"I'm pressed for time. Do you mind if I move in today?" Ann asked, thrilled at the opportunity and her good fortune. She had left her belongings in a friend's dorm temporarily until she found a room.

The days passed quickly, and the room proved to provide all the comforts of home. She loved her privacy and the warmth that greeted her every time she returned home. The aroma of lavender seemed very strong at times, and she imagined that the spirit of her beloved great-grandmother, Annie Buchannen, for whom she was named, permeated the room. But for some reason she felt that she shouldn't stay there. Once when she returned from a difficult day of classes, she was surprised to sense an urgent feeling to leave the apartment. She couldn't imagine why she was having those thoughts.

Other strange things happened in the apartment. It always seemed to be when she was in a bad mood or had had a trying day. At those times the aroma of lavender always permeated the room. It was unusual to her, but gave her comfort. Sometimes she'd even sense the presence of her great-grandmother. At those times it seemed that she was trying to tell Ann something, but

Ann didn't know what. Other times she'd wake up out of a deep
sleep having dreamt of her great-grandmother. She had always
remembered her as a kind, soft, loving woman with beautiful
white hair.

Ann had the sense that her great-grandmother was trying to
tell her to move out of the apartment. She didn't know what to
make of the occurrences, so she just accepted them and tried to
ignore the suggestions. The last thing she wanted was to move.
But when the aroma of lavender grew stronger, so did the message.
She must move. Her dreams grew more frequent and had grown
into nightmares. The messages from her great-grandmother were
stronger with each successive time.

One day in March she awoke with a tremendous feeling of
foreboding—stronger than ever before. This time she couldn't
ignore it. She sensed something was terribly wrong, and although
she didn't know what was going to happen, she suddenly felt
compelled to move out of the apartment as soon as possible. That
day. The messages just kept bombarding her without stopping.
She was sure it was her great-grandmother's spirit trying to
communicate with her. She didn't know what to do. She had no
where to go.

As soon as her first class was over, she scanned the bulletin
boards and began inquiring about other apartments. She had to
move out that day. This was all she knew. No matter where it
was. The little apartment where she had felt so safe was suddenly
a trap, an evil snare.

By noon she was in a panic that she couldn't explain. All
she knew was that she had to get out. She skipped two classes
and packed everything in a furry, hoping one of the leads from
the bulletin board would open up for her. She had been lucky to
sublet her apartment to a fellow she had met just the week before.
After looking at the apartment, he said he liked it on the spot.

Much to her relief, he said he'd move in that afternoon.

The only apartment she could find on such short notice was one across campus with dingy yellow walls and a brown metal bed. A two-burner stove and sink substituted for a kitchen. She couldn't believe that she was giving up the darling apartment for that, but she was determined to listen to her gut feelings, and of course, Annie Buchanan.

Her new tenant helped her move her things, and they dumped them in the middle of the room for the time being. She knew it would take her several days to arrange her belongings and try to make some semblance of homeyness in the cold room.

All evening Ann just wanted to cry as she scanned the bare walls, not really understanding what was going on. She could barely bring herself to arrange her books and other belongings in this dreary place. She had cleaned and scoured just about every inch, but it still seemed dirty. She fell into bed exhausted from the day's activities.

Two days later she ran into the young man who sublet her apartment. When he spotted her, he rushed up to her in a panic. The night before at 2:00 a.m., the apartment had caught on fire, and if he hadn't worked late, he might have died in the blaze. It seemed as if the cause was faulty wiring in the air conditioning unit's compressor. The apartment had burst into flames. The rest of the home had been spared any damage, thanks to the immediate response of the fire fighters. The new tenant, however, had lost most of his belongings and his expensive stereo equipment.

Ann couldn't believe her ears. She was terribly upset to hear the news and sorry that the young man had lost his possessions. But she knew, without a doubt, that she might have died because she would have been sleeping at the time the fire broke out. Her premonition and directions from her great-grandmother, Annie Buchanan, had saved her life.

THE WOMAN AND THE EIGHTEEN WHEELER
LYNN, ALABAMA

There is a stretch of road along Highway 5 heading toward Jasper near the towns of Natural Bridge, and Lynn, Alabama, where one foggy night in 1990 a terrible accident occurred. A young couple pulled their beat-up Buick off the road and began arguing. In a fit of fury, the man struck the woman, and she jumped out of the automobile and ran across the road toward the restaurant and truck stop for safety. But before she reached the other side of the road, an eighteen-wheeler rounded the bend in the road at top speed and struck her. The woman was killed instantly.

Ever since that tragic night, the local townspeople try to avoid that stretch of road after dark. Many have witnessed the appearance of a young woman waving her arms and walking along the road. She appears out of nowhere in the glow of their headlights. Whenever they stop to see if she needs help, the woman disappears into thin air. They say that the woman is the same person who was killed instantly in the accident.

TENNESSEE

THE FORTUNE TELLER
COVE CREEK, TENNESSEE

Mrs. Gladdys Lazette was a fortune teller and psychic in the 1890s in north Tennessee. She was so gifted in telling the future that people often asked her advice when making major decisions. They asked her opinion on marriage partners, business changes and the course of sickness and good health. Occasionally, the sheriff asked her to solve mysterious crimes and to locate missing people.

In Cove Creek, a small community on the banks of the Clinch River in east Tennessee, there had been a terrible timbering accident. A man who had been riding the logs down the river to the saw mill lost his footing. After stumbling for several seconds, he fell headfirst into the deepest part of the river. The other loggers tried to grab his hands when their logs passed by him, but the current that day was too strong and swept him quickly out of their grasp. Helpless, the men could only shout directions as they watched the victim struggle to keep afloat and try to catch log after log. The fallen logger was carried by the raging current for almost two miles downriver. Still unable to help him, the loggers watched with dread as he disappeared out of sight. For several days afterward, every man, woman and child from the small community searched, without success, the river and its banks for his body.

Desperate to find their friend, the loggers begged Mrs. Lazette to help them locate his body or tell them whether he was still alive. After some thought the psychic informed them that the body was still moving. She didn't know anything more and asked if they could come back the next day. The grief stricken loggers grumbled about the confusion and delay, but did as they were told and anxiously returned the next day. To their dismay, she didn't have any information the second day either, and she again asked them to return the following day, saying, "The body is still moving."

Some loggers said that she was a quack and that they should forget the idea. But others reluctantly agreed to return the following day, thinking that they didn't have anything to lose.

On the third day the skeptical men returned again for advice. This time Mrs. Lazette directed them to follow the road next to the river until they came to a large white house on a high hill, overlooking a square wooden platform that was used as a boat landing. She told them that a huge oak tree grew out of the river bank there, next to the dock. "You'll find his body in the river caught under the roots of that giant oak tree," she said sadly.

Immediately, the men went out to look for the body. To their great surprise and relief, they found the body of their friend exactly where she told them it would be, caught in the roots of that ancient oak tree.

THE UNBORN CHILD
TENNESSEE

An elderly woman began sewing clothes in anticipation of her first grandchild. When she had finished the newborn layette, she enthusiastically designed clothes for a six-month-old baby and then an older child, trying to imagine who her grandbaby would resemble.

Her daughter, Suellen, came to her in tears one day and begged her to stop. "My baby is not going to live, Mama," she said, wringing her hands.

The mother insisted that Suellen was just feeling a little depressed about being pregnant. She refused to believe her daughter and continued to sew darling, hand-smocked suits and other outfits to be used by a young toddler.

But the daughter kept insisting that her unborn baby would die.

"The clothes will never be worn," Suellen warned her mother again and again, the tragic idea overshadowing Suellen's every waking moment.

The doctor assured Suellen and her mother that the baby was very healthy. "There is no reason to believe that there will be any problems," the doctor declared. But the young girl still warned them that her baby would die, swearing that it would never live to even be six months of age.

Knowing the girl's fear, the doctor planned to take the baby by Cesarean section to ensure that nothing untoward would happen. Suellen went into labor several days before expected, however, and her own doctor was out of town. The doctor on call couldn't imagine why a Cesarean section was indicated, so he refused to perform one. But the labor was long and difficult. After Suellen had been in labor for many hours and still hadn't delivered, the doctor rushed to perform the Cesarean section. But by that time it was too late. The baby's position prevented a safe delivery, and the baby died.

After so much stress, the weakened mother began slipping away as her body fought a raging infection and complications of the delivery. For several days the doctors worried about losing the mother, too. The grief-stricken young woman finally overcame her physical illnesses, but never got over the death of her only baby.

THE CONFEDERATE SPY

SHARPS CHAPEL, TENNESSEE

In 1863 when a small detachment of Confederate soldiers arrived in the Tennessee mountain community of Sharps Chapel, they encountered a handful of men in their fifties who hadn't attached themselves to either side of the war. Many counties in Tennessee never seceded from the Union nor endorsed the Union cause. So finding farmers working in their own fields during the War Between the States was common in the hills of the border state, Tennessee. The men of Loyston, in Union County, wanted to remain neutral. But the soldiers refused to listen to them. At gun point and under the threat of death, the Confederate soldiers forced the civilians to join the Confederate Army.

Little did the Confederates know that these men had been acting as spies for the Confederacy all along, scouting out the positions of the Union Army and identifying Union sympathizers.

Bayless Burnett was suspected of being a Confederate spy by some, and others claim that he was a Union spy. No one knows for sure. All that is known is that his family claimed the last time they saw him alive, he left home carrying an ax, on his way to a house raising. No trace of his body was ever found. Some speculate that he was intercepted by the Confederate soldiers who had been seen in the area that day. Some believe that he was killed by the Union sympathizers for being a Confederate spy. His family prefers to believe he was killed for his horse.

One night several months after Bayless's disappearance, there was a terrible thunderstorm. His youngest son raced out into the night to gather the animals into the barn. The animals had sought refuge down in the lush bottom of their valley and

THE SPIRIT OF THE CONFEDERATE SPY FOLLOWS THE FENCE LINE

hovered under the dense trees for protection, but that was the worst place for them during a storm. The family had also dug their well in the same bottom, a spot where a spring of water gushed naturally up out of the ground. The son reached the well, and as he tried to shoo the animals homeward, he watched in terror as a waving light resembling a lantern sprang out of the well and moved swiftly, bobbing along the cow path as if someone was carrying it. The soft drizzle of rain freshened everything in sight and released the musty smell of wet earth. But the rain didn't stop the glimmering ball of light as it paused and hovered every few feet just above the ground about waist high, as if someone were stopping to catch his breath. Bayless's son saw it scurry up the steep hill to the ridge high above the farm. Ignoring his fears, he scrambled up the steep incline pursuing the light, hollering for it to stop. But when the light reached the crossed fences that marked the edge of Bayless's property, it disappeared completely, without a sound or even the faint marking of a footprint. Bayless's son told his family later that the shadow resembled a man running across the hill, carrying a swinging lantern.

The vision of that light popping out of the well and moving rapidly across the ridge occurred on several consecutive nights; but the son never identified the person or the source of the light. Each time the son was within a few feet of the light, it simply vanished, without a trace or the sound of footsteps.

The same vision appeared often, maybe once or twice a month. After the sixth or seventh time, other family members witnessed the light as well. Perplexed, the family wondered if maybe Bayless was trying to tell them what happened to him and where to look for his body. The son and others searched the hillside and dug everywhere, thinking that Bayless might have been buried there. They searched the bottom of the well and even dug deep trenches around the corners of the property where the light disappeared, but they never found Bayless's body or any evidence that anyone had ever been there.

Even to this day, in the spring of the year around the time of Bayless Burnett's disappearance, when the sky is moonless and as black as tar, a light can be seen erupting out of the old abandoned well, now long hidden among the brambles of the bottom land. The light continues its course, racing up the steep incline to that ridge above the farm. When the light reaches the decayed cross timbers of the fence line, it vanishes into the darkness, without a trace.

THE FAMILY BIBLE

KNOXVILLE, TENNESSEE

After a torrential rain Kim was called to her mother's home because water was pouring into the basement. Immediately the two women rushed to mop up the muddy water before it caused any damage and laid out to dry many of the stored items. Several days later they discovered a box of very old books sitting on the bottom shelf of an old cabinet. Much to their dismay, the box was falling apart from water damage, and the books inside were soaked and had begun to mildew. Kim and her mother felt heartsick because these were old family books that had been put away for safekeeping and, unfortunately, forgotten.

Carefully they lifted each book out of the carton, wiped it off as best as they could and laid it open on a nearby table to dry. When their job was almost done, Kim's mother heaved a disappointed sigh as she pulled her own family Bible out of the bottom.

"Oh, Mama! I'm so sorry," Kim said, not wanting to see the anguish in her mother's eyes.

But as she watched her mother caress the brown leather cover, she realized that the Bible was untouched. No mildew marred the binding; no moisture glued the pages together; and the printed pages were as crisp and dry as if they had been kept in a hot attic. The names of the great-grandparents and their children were still clear and legible.

The two marveled at the Bible's condition, especially when the bottom of the box was soaked through and fell apart when touched. All the other books in the box were completely ruined.

To this day Kim keeps the family Bible on the top shelf of her own collection of books for safekeeping. Every time she sees the book, she marvels at the tiny miracle that happened in her mother's basement.

WEST VIRGINIA

THE HAWTHORN HOUSE
SUMMIT POINT, WEST VIRGINIA

The young couple, Mauriel and Rick Joslyn, weren't at all suspicious about renting the Hawthorn House in Summit Point, West Virignia, even though the caretaker refused to spend even one night in the two-story structure.

He claimed that the mysterious noises terrified him. "They would frighten anyone in their right mind," he insisted.

The Hawthorn House, a beautiful 1795, black walnut log home with stucco exterior, was fully furnished with museum quality antiques. There was no mistake; providence had fallen in the Joslyns' laps. The rent was even less than they ever expected to pay in the small farm town of Summit Point. They had heard the stories about the caretaker refusing to spend a single night on the farm because of all the strange noises. But since they didn't believe in ghosts or anything supernatural, they immediately dismissed the warnings. Good Christian folks, the Joslyns didn't think that anything supernatural would bother them.

Mauriel and Rick moved into the house with their seven-year-old son, Nicholas, and six-month-old son, Alex. They immediately fell in love with the wide pine floors, high ceilings and lovely antiques. The house was built by Rev. Throckmorton, an Episcopal minister, and his wife who had immigrated to the small town from England. The Joslyns' couldn't miss the portrait in oil of Rev. Throckmorton hanging in the upstairs hall. Their son, Nicholas, was immediately curious about the serious, but not unkind, face that stared down at him every day. The picture had been painted by an itinerant painter in the early 1800s.

A Form in the Hall

The first night they spent in the house there was a fierce thunderstorm. Rick got up to close the windows so the rain wouldn't blow in and was about to go into the baby's room to close his window when he thought he saw Mauriel pass behind him heading in that direction. When he returned to bed, he realized that she hadn't even awakened. Immediately, he wondered who might have passed by him in the night. He got up and walked slowly into the baby's room and saw that the window had been closed already. The baby was sleeping peacefully with all his covers pulled up over him. He returned to bed but always wondered who the image was that he saw pass by him.

The Open Door

Several weeks elapsed without incident. Then one day when Mauriel returned home after being away all day, she discovered the door leading to the upstairs's porch standing wide open. Freezing cold air blew fiercely into the hallway. She closed the door as tightly as she could only to return again several times that day to find it again standing wide open. There was no lock, but the latch should have been sufficient to keep the door closed tight. This phenomenon happened repeatedly for the next few weeks. Mauriel became so exasperated that she finally just yelled into the hall, "Please, whoever you are. Please, leave this door closed. We're losing too much heat, and we're all going to die of pneumonia." From that day on, she never found the door open again.

THE HAWTHORN HOUSE

THE BABY IN THE CRIB

On another occasion Mauriel and Rick had been painting for a long time in the kitchen when Mauriel realized that she had left the baby asleep in the living room on a blanket on the floor. The baby couldn't crawl yet, but she went to check on him anyhow. Much to her dismay she found him missing. She and Rick searched the house frantically, only to discover him sleeping peacefully in his crib with his covers pulled up over him. Neither had brought him upstairs, and their other son denied taking his brother to bed.

REV. THROCKMORTON

Once, Mauriel had gone outside to hang up the laundry. The baby was asleep in his crib, and her son, Nick, was playing in his room. Suddenly Nick heard footsteps out in the hall and went to see if his mother had returned. Later he told his mother that he saw a man standing at the end of the hall by the entrance to the porch. The man looked exactly like Rev. Throckmorton. After that incident he never wanted to be in the house alone, not even for a minute.

TEXAS

THE MYSTERY OF THE GRAVE STONE
LIVINGSTON, TEXAS

In 1994 four Texans from the Ike Turner camp of the Sons of Confederate Veterans approached the Morning Dove Cemetery on the outskirts of town with misgivings. They wondered if they would ever find the exact location of Sgt. Thomas Gray's unmarked grave. During the previous three years, the Ike Turner Camp placed more than 240 marble monuments on unmarked Texas veterans' graves in Houston and surrounding areas. Their missions were never routine, but they didn't expect the intervention to come from the mysterious appearance of a supernatural force.

In the case of Sgt. Thomas Gray, the U.S. Census death records confirmed that he had been buried somewhere in the Morning Dove Cemetery. But when the men ordered the stone from the Federal Government, they still had not discovered the location of his grave or identified a marker for his family that might prove that he had actually been buried there. In other searches for the exact grave location, the original cemetery records often identified the place of burial in a family plot. But, unfortunately, the original records for the Morning Dove Cemetery had been lost.

The faces of the men were somber that hot July morning as they opened the six-foot-tall, spiked, wrought iron gates and entered the cemetery. The sound of their boots on the brick pavement echoed loudly, disrupting the morning stillness and causing the chatter of the birds to cease. The men hoped to finish this business before the heat of the day interrupted their mission. After looking around, they realized most of the headstones were ancient, dating back to the 1860s. The names and dates had been worn almost smooth by the passage of time and weather, making them difficult to read. Weeds, ivy and honeysuckle vines grew into a wild tangled shroud covering and almost obliterating neglected plots.

After some discussion the four Texans decided to split up. Each began his arduous search from the opposite corners of the cemetery, systematically examining each headstone in every row for a clue.

About an hour later, the four men had criss-crossed the cemetery without any luck. Perspiration dripped from their brows, and wearily, they removed their white ten-gallon hats to wipe it away. They wondered whether they would ever find the exact location. Trying to figure out what to do next, they paused for a rejuvenating drink of water from their canteens.

Several of the Texans were ready to give up and wanted to place the stone under two giant cedars in one remote corner of the cemetery, as a memorial to the veteran. It was a peaceful location and one the soldier might be proud of. There was some opposition, but in the end they all agreed, not knowing what else to do.

Just as two of the Texans placed the engraved square of marble at the base of the largest cedar, Charlie, another member of the group, standing about twenty paces away, hollered, "Wait!"

Charlie experienced a powerful supernatural force pulling him to the right of where he was standing. He had no choice but to follow its direction. After he moved ten paces to the right, the mysterious energy vanished. Struck as if dumb and visibly shaken from the experience, Charlie couldn't move from the spot. But before he collected his wits, the same energy drew him in another direction. After being pushed forward several feet, he was forced to reach down, down far enough to touch the ground. The other men watching Charlie reacted to the confusion by mumbling to themselves, not knowing what was going on.

At Charlie's feet lay a marble tombstone covered in a light layer of dirt, hiding the face from view. When he and two of his partners picked it up, the underside revealed the indentations of names and dates. They decided to take a chance and wash the surface free of mud. Even after cleaning the headstone, reading the inscription took some time. Carefully, the men traced the letters with their fingers and recognized the barely discernible name of Sarah Gray and her birth and death dates, which closely coincided with Thomas Gray's. To the right of the marker lay a large vacant spot the size of a coffin. The men concluded that this vacant spot must be Sgt. Thomas Gray's grave and placed the marble marker next to Sarah's. They assumed that Sarah had been his wife.

The Texans congratulated themselves on a job well done. But they couldn't have finished the task without the help from Sarah or perhaps from the spirit of Thomas.

Several days later two of the Texans from the crew returned to the spot with two other men from their S.C.V. camp. The Texans had been amazed by the episode and excitedly related the story to the others, showing them the location of Sarah's and Thomas's tombstones. To their amazement, Sarah's stone was then almost as clean as the new monument. The letters appeared more vivid. Was it possible for them to be etched deeper? Charlie could clearly read the name and dates without his glasses this time, something he couldn't do before. Even the small inscription at the bottom was now clearly visible, where in the beginning, the letters were too worn for any of the men to read.

Charlie tried to discount the episode by saying that the sun was shining directly on the stone this time. But the others knew for a fact that they had great difficulty reading Sarah's name the first time. For a while the men weren't even sure the inscription said Sarah. Now it looked as if someone had carved the letters deeper and even polished the face of the stone.

This mystery has touched every member of the camp.

The Sons of Confederate Veterans continue in their noble struggle of providing tombstones for unmarked Texans' graves, determined that none shall have died in vain and the memory of each be identified, revered and respected.

THE LONELY STRETCH OF ROAD
HOUSTON, TEXAS

In 1986 a couple in their fifties were traveling to Texas during the holidays to visit with their daughter. They had only two hours left in the long sixteen-hour trip from Atlanta, Georgia, and began to get excited. Just as they were changing lanes to the right, they watched, helpless, as an eighteen wheeler jumped the median strip and barreled down on them about to smash their Toyota. There was no way they could avoid this collision. All Mary could do was pray.

The right shoulder of the road dropped down at least ten feet, maybe more, into a deep ravine edged by towering pines. In the seconds that followed, Mary and her husband braced themselves for the impact. Mary instinctively held her arms over her husband, covering his head for protection. The gigantic eighteen wheeler struck their Toyota on the left side. With the first impact, the windshield shattered into a million pieces, she remembered. But miraculously, it held its shape.

Their little Toyota rolled over like a toy ball and spun around. Through a crack in the glass they watched the tractor-trailer swing back across the median strip and collide with another automobile. Then it recoiled, returning to their side of the road and careened into the couple's Toyota for a second time, demolishing the entire right side and immobilizing both doors. All the windows in the car were completely shattered. With that last impact their car rolled over several times before crashing down into a ravine. Mary said the experience was like being on one of those rides at the amusement park. All they could do was hold their breath and be thankful they were wearing seat belts.

With each roll of the car, Mary prayed, "Please, God, let us land on our wheels."

She remembers praying this over and over and over again, as many times as their car rolled over.

When the automobile finally stopped rolling, it had landed upright, but at the bottom of a thirty-foot embankment.

Mary impulsively tried to get out of her side, but the doors were crushed. She sat back in a daze trying to see through her dizziness and pain. She checked her body all over for injuries and seemed okay except for many tiny cuts from the glass and bruises she could feel on her arms and legs. She brushed away the glass, released her seat belt and sighed with relief after she moved all her limbs. She quickly examined her husband, and from what she could see, he suffered only a large gash on his forehead, but this was bleeding profusely. She vaguely remembers a voice telling her to open the door. She whispered for him to open his door and get out. She remembers helping him with his seat belt and quietly telling him to just push the door open. The voice seemed to come to her out of nowhere and repeated the command again, "Push the door open and get out." With a little shove from her, his door opened immediately, and they escaped. Once outside, they realized that their injuries were indeed minor. Afraid the car might catch fire any minute, they struggled to help each other climb up the steep, grassy embankment. Luckily, when they looked at the passengers in the truck and other automobile, no one had been killed. Not long afterwards, police sirens echoed in the still night air.

About an hour later, in the emergency room, the policeman questioned them about the accident.

"How did you get out of the car? Did you crawl out the

window?" the policeman asked.

Mary couldn't understand what he was talking about. The windows had been shattered. "If we had crawled out the window, we would have been cut up from all the glass. We just opened the door and got out," Mary said, and her husband agreed.

The policeman shook his head and looked at them with an expression of disbelief on his face. "Ma'am," he said, "you couldn't have gotten out of the automobile that way because both doors were welded shut from the impact of the collision. There were no openings in the windows either."

"Well," Mary said, "just look at us. That's how we got out. There wasn't any other way."

All she remembered at the time was the voice telling her to open the car door, and she followed the order. It did not make sense, but she thinks that the voice was from an angel of the Lord.

LELA
EL PASO, TEXAS

In 1970 Kathryn was diagnosed with cancer. During her chemotherapy treatments she became extremely ill and was hospitalized. When she was returning to her room one morning, she saw the figure of an old black woman standing quietly in the corner, just staring at her. Kathryn recognized the woman as her childhood nanny, Lela. Lela had taken care of Kathryn ever since she was born, and Kathryn was shocked to see her. The old woman began to beckon to Kathryn to come with her, but Kathryn wasn't ready and said, "No, Lela, I'm not ready. No! Lela, I'm not coming." Kathryn was filled with the old feelings of guilt that she had felt as a child when she defied Lela and wondered why Lela was calling her home. But Kathryn asserted herself again and refused to go. Finally, the old woman disappeared, but Kathryn never forgot the incident.

Kathryn has been free from cancer ever since. However, after that incident, every time she became seriously ill and was admitted to the hospital, she saw Lela appear, standing in the corner, beckoning to her. Kathryn refused to go each time, just the way she refused the first time.

Kathryn wasn't ever afraid because Lela had been a loving surrogate mother. All she ever felt from the woman was affection, and she regarded Lela as a mother, even though her own mother was a strong presence in her life. Lela kissed all her hurts, nursed her when she was sick and attended to her every childhood need.

Kathryn knows that when it's her time to go, Lela will be there for her, beckoning for her to go, and this thought gives her comfort.

SUPERNATURAL

St. Patrick's Cathedral

ST. PATRICK'S CATHEDRAL
NEW YORK CITY, NEW YORK

In September, 1994, Judy Waldorf, a resident of Macon, Georgia, and wife of a Methodist minister, traveled to New York City for pleasure and to tour the sights. While on her visit she snapped a picture of St. Patrick's Cathedral. Impressed by the building's ornate, stone carvings and towering spires that rose high into the air, she wanted to capture its beauty forever.

Later, when Judy returned home and examined her developed pictures, she discovered the ghostlike, white silhouette of the Cathedral in the spot where the building stood. The front of St. Patrick's had been completely obliterated. Disappointed, she checked the negative, thinking that this mishap had occurred during the developing process, but much to her dismay, she discovered that the image of the cathedral had been completely wiped out there also. She was stunned because the other parts of the photo duplicated completely the scene she thought she photographed.

Some people claim that the white silhouette was caused by the reflection of the sun, but others think that it was the bright illumination of God's dazzling light radiating from the church. They think that the cathedral's aura was so brilliant that it actually blocked out the complete shape of the famous house of God. If the sun had been the culprit, the trees, buses and other objects in the photo would also have been blotted out, but they weren't.

THE HOSPITAL AT GETTYSBURG
GETTYSBURG, PENNSYLVANIA

History has a way of clinging to the buildings and land where tragic events have occurred, haunting them forever. The battlefield at Gettysburg, Pennsylvania, now a national park and historic site, is one of those places. The decisive battle in the War Between the States at Gettysburg has long been noted by historians as the turning point of the war. The mere mention of the name Gettysburg conjures up mental images of death, destruction and a tragic defeat for the South. After thousands of both Union and Confederate soldiers met their deaths, many consider the grounds of the battlefield hallowed, even sacred; others swear they are haunted by the armies of the North and South.

The Johnson couple wasn't at all worried about buying the colonial stone house and two hundred acres of land adjoining the Gettysburg Battlefield. The two looked forward to riding their horses across the trails maintained by the park service.

When told that the house had been used as a hospital during the war, the Johnsons decided to research the former hospital's past. Much to their surprise they discovered that their formal living room had been used as the surgery. They read eye-witness accounts of the surgical amputations, accounts of arms and legs being thrown out their living room window until the stack was too tall to accept any more. Tales of the unbearable stench and of unchecked pestilence raging among the wounded soldiers were common. But in the 1860s hospital staffs and doctors didn't know how to prevent the spread of disease. Other accounts reported dead horses piled up and burned behind the barn in a deep ditch. The Johnson's garden is now located in that same spot. Occasionally, the earth produces part of a bone or buckle from a bridle that has worked its way up to the surface. The Johnsons pushed the gruesome details to the back of their minds and made the house into a home.

George dreamed of riding horses, and Sarah of raising sheep. After a few years their dreams were fulfilled. George owned several beautiful Arabian horses, and together he and Sarah raised over a hundred sheep.

The Johnsons had forgotten the history of the dwelling as a hospital until one sweltering July day. Sarah went out into the garden shed to get some tomatoes for lunch. Just outside the kitchen door, she felt a frigid chill in the air and wondered whether a storm was coming. She looked at the sky, but it was clear, just as blue as a robin's egg. When she reached the shed only ten feet from the kitchen door, the temperature had grown even colder. She turned abruptly, forgetting her tomatoes, frightened by something she couldn't explain. She wanted desperately to return to the house. Much to her surprise, a tall, handsome figure of a Confederate soldier in full dress uniform stood in her way. He peered down at her with the kindest expression she had ever seen. When she looked into his eyes, immediately, all her fears left her.

Sarah said later that she'd never forget the sight of his gray felt hat decorated with a huge black ostrich feather. A golden, satin sash wrapped the waist of his gray wool uniform. The fringe of the sash hung down to just above the edge of his knee-high leather boots. A silver and gold sword hung loosely at his side, and his hand curved casually around the handle. Wide gold braid decorated his sleeves in large oval circles, telling her that he was an officer, maybe even a general.

Not knowing what to do, she pushed past him and returned

THE HOSPTIAL AT GETTYSBURG

to the kitchen without the tomatoes, her hands trembling, her face ashen.

"Where are the tomatoes?" Ann asked, very frustrated because she had been waiting for them. When Ann saw her mother's face, she knew immediately that something was wrong. But her mother never said a word and sat down stiffly in the nearest chair, her heart still pounding from the shock.

Ann raced out the door, frantic to see what had affected her mother so strangely. She had taken only three steps when she saw the same Confederate soldier towering above her. He smiled down at her, too, and said, "Don't be afraid. I won't hurt you."

Ann returned to the kitchen just as shaken as her mother. But she never forgot his handsome face, heavy brown beard and kind azure eyes.

Later, when the two women described the soldier to George and others, they all decided the ghost must have been Major General "J.E.B." Stuart of the Confederate cavalry. He led a fierce attack against the right flank of the Union line.

On July 1st., 2nd. and 3rd., 1863, "J.E.B." Stuart and his men fought all around the Johnson farm, trying to secure the Baltimore Turnpike as a supply line and escape route. Many of J.E.B.'s friends died at Gettysburg, and many lay wounded in the hospital for months afterward.

J.E.B. Stuart didn't die until May 12, 1864, in Richmond. But numerous accounts state that Maj. Gen. Stuart's black plume was clearly visible from a good distance in every battle he fought. It was his insignia. He was earnest in his endeavors, devoted to the cause and loved his men and his country.

From a picture, Sarah and Ann positively identified the ghost they saw as J.E.B Stuart. They never saw him again, but the idea that he had returned to the site of a fierce battle to check on his men enhanced their impression of him. They feel safe, imagining that his spirit lingers somewhere nearby even now.

THE ANGEL BIRD
GRAY, GEORGIA

In November 1995, while Gene Chodkiewicz was walking along the busy street near his antique shop, a sparrow flew directly to his feet. Without thinking, he reached down with a cupped hand, and the bird jumped into the center of his palm. He brought the bird up to his chest and gently stroked its head for a moment, but after a few seconds the bird flew away.

Later, he told the story to his friend, and she thought the bird was an angel bringing him a message and that he'd hear more soon.

Two weeks later a stranger came into his antique store and brought him four bird prints.

The stranger said, "We've had these prints for years and have no use for them anymore, so we've decided to give them to you."

Because the prints were so lovely, Mr. Chodkiewicz offered to pay the man for them, but the man refused. After the stranger left, Gene and a friend, another antique dealer, examined the prints and realized that they were rare nineteenth-century etchings, dated around 1860. He estimated their value to be more than $100 each. The donor had disappeared, and Gene didn't know where to contact him.

Strangely enough, that day was the wedding anniversary of his marriage with his beloved first wife, who had passed away in 1971. All her life she had loved birds with an undying passion.

FLYING ANGEL
MILLEDGEVILLE, GEORGIA

Mrs. Stewart is a ninety-two-year-old resident living in Mrs. Brantley's retirement home. She was returning to her room from breakfast one morning in the spring of 1996 when something made her look up at the ceiling. She spotted an object flying toward her, it came very fast and as straight as an arrow, and it appeared to be the size of a dinner plate. It came so quickly that she could barely make out what it looked like, but she knew it had wings. She turned around and watched it round the corner to the front of the building. Something told her that it was an angel of the Lord. She knew this with certainty. Also, she knew the vision was meant for her because she had been alone in the hall; otherwise it wouldn't have picked the time she was returning from the dining hall.

At the time she witnessed the angel, she didn't know that one of her neighbors had passed away. She didn't find out about this until 11:00 a.m. that same morning. But this was the most wonderful experience she'd ever had and she knew she'd never forget it. For some reason the Lord wanted her to see this angel, and she would always be grateful.

THE MYSTERIOUS STRANGER
MILLEDGEVILLE, GEORGIA

In 1992 the youngest of five very active children escaped from the confines of the kitchen before the mother knew what had happened. When she realized that he had disappeared, she frantically searched the entire house without finding a trace of her son's tiny blond-haired form racing in the opposite direction. She ran out to the back yard thinking that the child had headed for the sandbox, but when she didn't find him, her pounding heart sank. It was hard for her to imagine that he had disappeared so fast.

She heard the front doorbell ring and flew to answer it, hoping the caller might help her search for her missing baby. When she opened the door, a very tall, thin-faced man stared down at her. He was carrying her child in his arms.

"He was in the middle of the street, Ma'am. I didn't want him to get hurt, so I picked him up," the man said with a kind smile on his face. "The boy pointed to this house. Is he your child?"

The mother grabbed her squirming son from the kind man's arms.

"Oh, yes," she said, hugging him for dear life and checking him all over to make sure he was all there.

"Yes, he's my baby. I've been looking for him every. . . ." The mother looked back at the man at the door to thank him, but the tall, thin stranger had vanished. She darted out into the yard, not wanting the man to get away without a thank you, but after peering up and down the street and scanning the neighbor's yards, she gave up. The mysterious stranger had disappeared without a trace.

All the way back to the house, the mother hugged her squirming son and thanked God for sending an angel that day to save him from harm.

THE MYSTERIOUS COLD SPOT
MILLEDGEVILLE, GEORGIA

Late one night the woman of the house put on a kettle of hot water for a cup of tea before she went to bed. But, unfortunately, she forgot about the boiling tea pot and went to sleep.

In the middle of the night, her daughter came in to wake her. "I'm freezing Mama. I need a blanket." When the woman woke up, she, too, was freezing from a draft of icy cold air that surrounded her and got up to get a blanket from the other side of the house. When she passed by the kitchen, she realized that she had left the stove on. The tin tea kettle was smoldering and warped beyond all recognition. She turned off the stove just in time to prevent a fire.

Fortunately, the draft of cold air had awakened them. When she checked her daughter's room, three blankets lay folded at the bottom of the bed. It still felt chilly in the room, but the temperature on the thermostat was 72 degrees. That draft of cold air had saved their life. Was it the actions of an angel or spirit? She has often wondered.

Other Books by Barbara Duffey

Banshees, Bugles and Belles: True Ghost Stories of Georgia

Valor and Lace: The Roles of Confederate Women 1861-1865
      Edited by Mauriel Phillips Joslyn
      Chapter Six - The Nurse
            Ella K. Newsom Trader
            By Barbara Duffey

BIBLIOGRAPHY

DESTREHAN PLANTATION
Levatino, Madeline. *Past Masters: The History and Hauntings of Destrehan Plantation.* New Orleans, Louisiana: Dinstuhl Printing and Publishing, 1991.
Gilger, Kristen. "Manor's Spirits Awake," *Times-Picayune.* New Orleans, Louisiana November 4, 1984.

THE LALAURIE HOUSE
Plume, Janet. "Mansion with a ghostly reputation for sale in Quarter for $1.9 million," *New Orleans Times-Picayune.* New Orleans, Louisiana November 12, 1988.

THE GHOSTS OF ROWAN OAK
Morris, Willie. "Faulkner's Mississippi," *The National Geographic Magazine.* Washington, D. C., Vol. 175 No. 3, March 1989, p 313-339.
Biggs, Jennifer. "Where Things go Bump in The Night," *The Clarion-Ledger.* Oxford, Mississippi Sunday, October 25, 1992, p 1F, 2F.

BEAUVOIR
Federal Writer's Project of the Works Progress Administration. *Mississippi: A guide to the Magnolia State.* New York: Hastings House, 1949, p 292-294.
Phillips, Herb. "Haunts." *The Clarion-Ledger.* Oxford, Mississippi October 28, 1990, p 2F.

THE TWISTED OAKS OF BILOXI
Archives of University of Mississippi, Specimen's of Mississippi Folklore by Palmer Hudson. Original manuscript.

McRAVEN
Stories from an interview with owner Leyland French.
Phillips, Herb. "Haunts." *The Clarion-Ledger.* Oxford, Mississippi October 28, 1990.

A UNION SOLDIER CALLS FROM HIS GRAVE
Kirkpatrick, Lil. "They said anything could happen and it did." *The Clarion-Ledger.* Oxford, Mississippi October 25, 1980.

BARNSLEY GARDENS AND ETERNAL LOVE
Cofer, Carl H. *The Barnsley Gardens Story.* Barnsley Gardens, Adairsville, Georgia 1992.
"Barnsley Gardens—A story of triumphs and tragedies." *Georgia Country Life Magazine.* Baxley, Georgia Summer 1996.
Courtesy of Dyan Nelson, Tour Guide at Barnsley Gardens.

Courtesy of Clent Coker, Historian at Barnsley Gardens.

THE 1848 HOUSE RESTAURANT
Courtesy of William B. Dunaway and interviews with members of the staff.
Historical Sketch and flyer written and printed by The 1848 House Restaurant and
Conference Center.

THE KENNESAW HOUSE
(1) Marietta Museum of History Handout.
(2) Pittenger, William. *The Great Locomotive Chase.* Philadelphia MCMXXI: The
Penn Publishing Co., 1889, p 86.
(3) Richard, Fraise J. *The Florence Nightingale of the Southern Army.* New York
and Baltimore: Broadway Publishing Co., 1914, p 49, 93, 95.
(4) Staff Reporter. "Spirits Linger in Legend and Sighting." *Newcomer's Guide.*
Marietta, Georgia July 22, 1990, 70g.
Joslyn, Mauriel Phillips; Duffey, Barbara. *Valor and Lace: The Roles of
Confederate Women 1861-1865.* Murfreesboro, TN: Southern Heritage Press,
1996.
Courtesy of Dan Cox, Marietta Museum of History.

GHOSTS INHABIT A BUILDING ON MARIETTA'S PUBLIC SQUARE
Story teller wishes to remain unnamed.

THE STORY OF THE BRUMBY ROCKER
Invisible Hands." *Marietta Journal.* November 8, 1888.

GENERAL WILLIAM T. SHERMAN'S ARMY
Courtesy of Virginia Davis.

THE PUBLIC HOUSE RESTAURANT
Courtesy of an interview with the manager and staff.
Stephens, Susan. *The Public House Restaurant.* Roswell, Georgia.

THE MYSTERIOUS CLOSET
THE VICTORIAN MIRROR
Courtesy of Susan Bagwell.

THE TUCKER-NEWSOM PLACE
Courtesy of previous owners, and staff of Hugs Restaurant.
Courtesy of Mr. Williams, Archivist of Madison.

SARAH'S WINGS
Courtesy of Thomas Jones and his family.

THE HOMESTEAD
Courtesy of Fielding D. Whipple.

THE GHOSTS OF LOCKERLY HALL

Courtesy of ECC International, Inc.
Courtesy of Diane Perdue, Guest House Manager.
Courtesy of John Adcock.
Courtesy of Sibley Jennings.
Courtesy of Mrs. Inman from Augusta.

THE LAST SUPPER

Courtesy of Barbara Duffey.

THE OLD STATE PRISON FARM

Courtesy of Larry Findley.

THE CEMETERY

Donor wishes to remain unnamed, but the story is true.

SISSY WILLIS—THE GHOST OF THE WILLIS HOUSE

Courtesy of Saralyn Latham.

THE NATIVITY SCENE

Courtesy of Barbara Duffey.
Duffey, Barbara. "The Nativity Scene." *The Union Recorder.* Milledgeville,
    Georgia December 25, 1993.

THE RILEY- WILLIAMS HOUSE

Courtesy of Zeke and Carol Williams.

DEMOSTHENIAN HALL

Courtesy of University of Georgia.
Courtesy of Mark Smith.

MIDWAY, GEORGIA
JOHN LAMBERT
A PATRIOTIC COW
THE SUICIDE
THE CRACK IN THE WALL
CHLOE
SYLVIA AND HER LOVER
A CHILD GHOST

Martin, Josephine Bacon. *Midway Georgia In History and Legend 1752-1867.*
    Midway, Georgia: The Midway Museum, Fifth Edition 1994.
Courtesy of Joann Clark and The Midway Society Museum.
Campbell, Connie Pfc. "Local fables haunt Midway, Halloween." *The Midway
    Patriot.* Thursday, Oct. 25, 1990.

THE COGDELL LIGHT

Courtesy of Dr. Robert Lott.

THE GHOSTS OF CUMBERLAND ISLAND
THE STAFFORD HOUSE
THE POLO PLAYER
THE OWLS AT DUNGENESS
PLUM ORCHARD
THE WOMAN IN WHITE

Rockefeller, Nancy Carnegie. *The Carnegies of Cumberland Island.* Camden
     County, Georgia, U.S.A., 1993. (Privately Printed)
From 1880 to the present an oral history of Cumberland Island developed by the
     National Park Service, courtesy of the National Park Service.
Courtesy of Joe Peacock.
Stepzinski, Teresa. "Coastal Georgia's Ghosts." *The Times Union.* Jacksonville,
     Florida Sunday October 29, 1995, p A 1, A 4.

THE LEGEND OF JACKSONBOROUGH'S CURSE

Douglas, Maria Neder. "The Town That Was Founded Because of a Curse," *Rural
     Georgia.* August 1986, p 2,5,10,22.

THE SPIRITS OF THE CEMETERY

Courtesy of Shirley Sanders, Los Angeles, Califonia.

LAVENDER ON THE PILLOW

Courtesy of Ann Buchannen Strickland.

THE WOMAN AND THE EIGHTEEN WHEELER

Courtesy of the people from Lynn, Alabama.

THE FORTUNE TELLER
THE UNBORN CHILD
THE CONFEDERATE SPY

Courtesy of Mary Lucik and her family.

THE FAMILY BIBLE

Courtesy of Kim Hutchens.

THE HAWTHORN HOUSE

Courtesy of Mauriel Joslyn and her family.

THE MYSTERY OF THE GRAVE STONE

Courtesy of Dr. Craig Reese.
Courtesy of Charlie Hubbard.

THE LONELY STRETCH OF ROAD

Courtesy of Millie Waltz.

LELA

Courtesy of Kathryn Kizziar.

SUPERNATURAL STORIES

THE HOSPITAL AT GETTYSBURG

Courtesy of Bill and Enid Craumer

ST. PATRICK'S CATHEDRAL

Courtesy of Judy Waldor, Macon Georgia.

THE ANGEL BIRD

Courtesy of Gene Chodkiewicz.

THE FLYING ANGEL

Courtesy of Mrs. Myrtle Stewart, Brantley's Retirement Home.

THE MYSTERIOUS STRANGER

Courtesy of an anonymous donor.

THE MYSTERIOUS COLD SPOT

Courtesy of Barbara Bassford.